Finding Your Funny Bone!

Finding Your Funny Bone!

The Actor's Guide to Physical Comedy and Characters

NANCY GOLD

A Smith and Kraus Book
Published by Smith and Kraus, Inc.
177 Lyme Road, Hanover, NH 03755
www.SmithandKraus.com

First Edition: June 2007
Manufactured in the United States of America
9 8 7 6 5 4 3 2 1

Cover design and book production by Julia Gignoux, Freedom Hill Design
Text design and formatting by Kate Mueller, Electric Dragon Productions

ISBN-13 978-1-57525-449-4
ISBN-10 1-57525-449-2
Library of Congress Control Number: 2007930045

To Lol Levy . . .

The Gift of Love and Laughter in my Life.

Contents

Acknowledgments

Thank You! Everyone who participated in the creation of this book.

Thank You! My family, friends, students, and teachers—to name you all would fill another book.

Thank You! Lol Levy, my soul partner in comedy, husband in life, graphic, computer, and production genius—I owe you a dollar.

Thank You! Dr. Jerome Gold, my father, for your love of life, laughter, and support. Betty Gold, my mother, for your eye for detail and support. Harriet Der Avedisian, my sister, for your creativity, logic, and support. Robert Der Avedisian, my brother-in-law, for your steaks and support.

Thank You! Mary Fran Loftus, Lauren Levian, Kristina Callahan, Michael Wolfson, Marti Cate, Joyce Tattelman, Dorothy Tyo, Cathy Wild, Ian Ruskin, Carol Murphy, Mitzie Abe, Merrinell Phillips, David Clifton Phillips, Debbie Cabin, Stan and Joel Friedman, Sharon Holley, Darryl Roberts, Nancy Leonard, and Bill "Moyni" Moynihan—my muses and supports.

Thank You! Sam and Grace Levy who have the clown blood in them.

Thank You! Craig Slaight for your kind words of encouragement and action on my behalf—and the American Conservatory Theater for your support.

Thank You! Rachel Fink, MaryBeth Cavanaugh, and the Berkeley Repertory Theatre for your support.

Thank You! Sally Repplier Evert, Kevin Berne, Alessandra Mello, Kate Mueller, and Julia Gignoux for putting the TAH DAH!!! in the book.

Thank You! Bari Rolfe for giving me the idea to write a book over a cheese sandwich.

Thank You! Peter Berke for combining the logic of science with the art of mime and juggling.

Thank You! Tyler Burns, Ron Campbell, Jake Chilcott, Donna Dahrouge, Olivia Scott Dahrouge, Theo Ephraim, Zoe Firth, George Killingsworth, Caroline Leibman, Grace Levy, Lol Levy, Sam Levy, Elvin McRae, Wendy Parkman, Alex Preston, CJ Preston, Hannah Ruskin, Ian Ruskin, Brian Degan Scott, Zack Scott, Haley Wild-Sichi, Cathy Wild, and Mr. Whimsy—for your talent, energy, and most of all . . . for putting your faces in the book.

Thank You! The Reader, for your courage and spirit of adventure in searching for a Funny Bone in the first place.

Foreword

I have been an enormous fan of Nancy Gold and her theater work for years. So much so, that upon first encountering her talents, I eagerly sought her as a master artist/teacher here at the American Conservatory Theater's Young Conservatory. A regular faculty member at the conservatory for many years now, Nancy continues to affect young actors with her artistry and her visionary teaching. In fact, it was a little over a year ago that I urged Nancy to allow me to approach Smith and Kraus Publishers with the idea of publishing a book highlighting the techniques she employs in her work. When they examined Nancy's work, Smith and Kraus were as eager as I was for such a book. And so, the book in your hand is the result.

A consummate theater artist, Nancy Gold has devoted her life to creating vibrant and imaginative theater. Because she has continued to return to the studio to refine and expand upon her techniques, the work Gold brings to any project or class is fresh, usable and electric. Throughout her professional life, Gold has devoted herself to her personal artistic evolution, from completing her professional master's level training at Ecole International du Theater Jacques LeCoq in Paris (working with the great master himself) to advanced studies in physical theater with the astonishing Czech director, Ctibor Turba.

Physical theater training is perhaps the most difficult training to capture within the pages of a book. Like ballet or singing training, it requires an immediate kinesthetic experience, best offered with corrections along the way. This is one of the reasons why *Finding Your Funny Bone! The Actor's Guide to Physical Comedy and*

Characters is so remarkable and such an accomplishment. It is as useful as it is illuminating. Rather than talk about the work, Gold insists that you jump in and try it on. It is also a real find for the performer or teacher, a treasured volume to include in the actors tool kit. With this book, the first to capture her techniques, Gold has gotten down to very specific areas of focus and offers the brilliant scheme for taking the performer on an experiential journey, a "Tour of Discovery," as she so enticingly puts it, in which she happily offers the player the opportunity to stop along the way. Without judgment, Gold encourages personal imprint and experimentation and gives permission to discard what doesn't suit the individual. This has been a key in her performance work and a large tribute to her success here at ACT. And while the pages that follow are filled with the technical language of bodywork and training, Gold isn't asking for anyone to pass some elusive scientific test. *Accessibility* is an important ingredient to Nancy Gold's work, and it is beautifully a part of this book. So many technique books appear as dogma, profound solo visions on a process that is never solo. Here, Gold asks for you to explore, experience, and make your own choice on what to take away. She is as interested in your *personal* journey, your needs, and the outcome of the course as she is in demanding you adhere to rigid formulas. What Gold has to offer represents significant lessons as building blocks; nonexclusive magnificent tatters that can help compose the symphony of your work.

When I first read this manuscript, I was struck with how much of the persona of Nancy Gold comes through in the writing. Happily, the voice in Gold's prose is the enthusiastic tone of discovery, offered as if you were the most trusted student, leaning forward, in her studio class. Gold is a masterful artist, who treasures the silliness that keeps one, finally, from becoming overly self-conscious. She enjoys the process of creation so much that you can't help but be caught up with her boundless positive sparkle while on this "tour." I encourage you to jump into her amazing book with both feet, as if you were to jump into your favorite dessert. Don't spare on the mouthfuls, the feeling you will have when finished will be not only useful in all your work, it will be life affirming. If you happen to be a teacher, looking for a resource to help you free up the physical constraints of your acting students, you couldn't be in better hands. We incorporate Gold's work in every session at ACT. I'm sure once you've encountered her gifts in these pages, you will too.

Craig Slaight
American Conservatory Theater
San Francisco, California

Introduction

The first time I heard the phrase, "How to Find Your Stupid and Stay in It," was at the International Clown Congress in Philadelphia. Pierre Byland said it as he was giving a workshop in clowning. It stuck to me like glue. What a perfect description of clowning and comedy!

Let's face it. No one wants to be considered stupid by others. It brings up painful ridicule and embarrassing moments filled with total frustration and illogical logic. It brings that voice in your head screaming into consciousness HOW STUPID CAN YOU GET! HOW COULD YOU DO SUCH A THING? YOU ARE SOOOOOO STUPID!

But when you think of comedy, that is exactly what happens. The comedian or clown has to find his or her stupid and stay in it for the audience to be reminded of their humanity. And it takes a great deal of courage, intelligence, and grace to stay stupid.

The following is a *guide* to finding your personal stupid and a *how to* approach for staying in it. This is geared for the performer, actor, speaker, and student of virtually anything. Stupid knows no bounds, and comedy is the sweet smile that makes your life more enjoyable.

This guide has taken years to realize. All the parts were floating around, but recently they landed in a fashion I could verbalize and communicate. Developing your Eye for how and what creates a certain affect and effect is all part of it. Develop your Eye—not only focus but also to see the world in a new way. See what works and how things can be more exciting. It's all right in front of your eyes. You just need to Look and See—fine-tune the tube or set the tracking or find the right website. There is all that beautiful information and clear pictures staring you right in the face.

Some people are naturals—they have the gift. Others need a little guidance. But either way, these games, exercises, improvisations, and entrées will enrich you on both the professional performance level and within yourself. So enjoy, whether you are 5 years old or 50 or have decided to team up with Jack Benny and remain 39 forever.

I love comedy. I remember watching those live television shows when I was very little. Danny Kaye and Carol Burnett would have their variety shows. I used to wait for those moments when something went wrong. A line was dropped or a door got stuck or they *lost it* and cracked up. Those wrong moments were the best right moments of the shows.

I loved to listen to the stand-up routines. How did they get those laughs? They just knew how to say their lines, tell their jokes, and quickly respond to whatever happened onstage and on-camera. There was no laugh track. It was real. There was an edge to it, because you couldn't yell cut—millions of viewers were watching. It was dangerous and delightful.

I wanted to be a comedian. I so admired stand-up comedy. But I personally did not possess the hard edge that stand-up requires. But the comic monologue or skit was right up my alley. What better thing to do than find that part of myself that was really other folks and copy or satirize them? Oh, the Marx Brothers and Bob Hope and Carol Burnett and Robin Williams and a long list of others charged me up. But how did they do it? They had the gift.

What was that magic they all had? And more important, how could I get some? So I took theater classes. I thought I needed to learn the Art of Acting. But I had difficulty with the Method. Just thinking and remembering things did not do it for me. I needed a more physical approach. I was playing the part of a young Indian girl. I had to be in pain because I was hungry and exhausted. As much as I thought about being hungry and exhausted, my life at that point had not paralleled my character's, and I couldn't muster up sufficient hunger and exhaustion. My director came over and squeezed my stomach 'til it hurt. From that moment, I had a physical memory to go on, and I didn't have to think about being hungry, I thought about my stomach getting squeezed. I think that was the first time I used an abstract approach to get a concrete result.

And that is what this guide will do for you. It will give you an abstract approach to achieving very specific concrete results. Basically, if you want to jump high, don't think about jumping or trying to get your body off the ground. Let go of the control and *allow* the string that grows at the top of your head pull you up and get pulled down into the center of the earth at the same time, and you'll be springing off the floor before you know it. Spontaneity can actually take a lot of technique to achieve. Some times you are conscious of it, and other times you just do it. For those times when you are conscious, here are some ways to just do it.

I wanted to do that. Make people laugh. Ever since I was seven. I thought it was stand-up comedy—but actually it was comedy in all its forms. I began with physical comedy. I saw the Art of Mime in High School. Claude Kipnis did a lecture demonstration, and I thought I'd fallen off a cliff. It was magical and funny and powerful and required only you and the air around you. There was a world out there where anything could happen. The only boundaries were what my body could do and what my imagination would think of. Mime was so magnificent. It was so independent. You didn't need anything—you had it All. All you needed was your Body and the Air around you! That air defined Space. That air was Space. What you needed was SPACE. Oh the joys of manipulating space. The Power of making something out of nothing. I was a magician, and I didn't know a thing about magic. I could make people gasp and laugh and feel and change.

Yeah, I needed to make them FEEL. Hmmm, here was a tricky thing. You see as a mime I was a master of illusion, imitation, re-creation. I could create the look of a feeling, but to create or actually experience a REAL feeling, well, that required REAL ACTING techniques. And now I was back to remembering my feelings, curing myself of the experience, and starting all over again with a fresh powerful memory. This went on for a while until I decided to focus on my mime career, because like a dancer, I figured I had only X amount of time, and then the body would not be as supple, and when that happened, I could focus on the acting. Acting you could do any time, but Mime, well, that had a limited shelf life.

So I asked my mentor, Claude Kipnis, what I should do, and he suggested I go to Jacques LeCoq in Paris. He taught more than manipulation. He taught theater. So I went.

Here is where I encountered Mime that was not the illusion type. Manipulation was broken down into sequences. Each movement could be divided into many movements, and depending on how you did them, slow, fast, big, small, you got a different effect.

Then I met Masks—all kinds of masks—neutral, character, utilitarian. WOW. Each movement was powerful, and the more focused you could get the better. Doing nothing was the most powerful thing you could do.

Kipnis had everyone start in zero position—which basically was aligning your body in a straight line. The neutral mask only worked if you were in zero position, but it required ultimate focus, no judgment, and filling your space with energy.

Add to this elements—Water, Wind, Fire, and Tree. Mix and match the elements on a bench, add degrees of each element, and voilá! You have a plethora of characters and relationships. Then broaden your horizons and make anything an element, and once again the world of performing was infinite.

Add color as emotions and color intensity as emotional expression from light pink to deep red, and you have a magnificent palate of feeling to pull from. No more guesswork. No more drudging and redrudging that illusive feeling: think of your element and color and your body knows. It goes to places your conscious mind would never dream of. Whew!

But something was still missing. I might be feeling and moving and picking symbols that my audience could relate to, but did my audience feel it? And I had to find out how I could adjust this enormously expressive face to fit in that little camera. I EXPLODED on film.

Other performers moved great and created brilliant stories. What did those magical variety artists like Bob Berky and Michael Moschen have that left their audiences standing on their feet? What did they possess that touched you deeply? What does Cirque du Soleil have, and Chagall and Van Gogh and Rodin?

And then I met Leonard Pitt. He had just got back from Bali where he studied mask theater. He did this little exercise he called Ghee Dong. BAM WHAM SLAM—YEAH!!! It was a very simple game of tossing ENERGY around like a laser beam. OHHH, it was fun. You could hit body parts, and it was like a cartoon. It looked great. It felt great to do. Felt in your whole body great . . . In fact, ENERGY was the key. This was science and art coming together. This was metaphysical meets Stanislavski. This was connecting the universe to your performance. Why stop at the world when you have unlimited energy available to use? Don Richardson, who was a television director and acting teacher, talked about how all emotions were actually created physiologically the same way in your body, and how you could walk looking down at tiles and counting them, and people would interpret your feeling in their perceived response to the action of the scene.

All of ART—no matter what kind it is—is an exchange of ENERGY between the audience and the artwork or performer, between the performers on the stage and between you as the performer and the character.

Eureka!!! Oh my God, there is a method to this madness.

And then came Madness to make the Method—in meeting and studying with Ctibor Turba. I first saw Turba in Paris. Not him personally, but his work. The giant rolls of Paper. The spontaneous stupidity, the illogical logic. I fell in love with his work. And then he came to America, and I got to study with the Paperman himself. Priceless information on the clown. And on being so in control out of control that you could laugh in increments that went from zero all the way to the extreme of laughter to the abstraction of laughter and back again, taking the same steps down that you took going up.

Apply what I coined as these CHROMATIC steps to physical and emotional expression, and guess what?! You put Space, Energy, Mime, Masks, Movement; add some Elements, Chromatic Movement, and Emotional Expression; top it off with some Clowning; mix in Relationship to inanimate Objects and Relationships to other Characters; and you have a *guide* to *how to* create comedy characters.

I once had a job as a tour guide for Sara Lee Bakeries. It was one way I subsidized my college education and my sweet tooth . . .

"Hello, my name is Nancy Gold, and I'd liked to welcome you to *Finding Your Funny Bone!* Please no touching the dough and don't miss the butter extruder."

WELCOME TO THE TOUR

The Tour consists of many stops, which will help you develop specific Tools that you can use to create comedy and characters. It is a Tour of Discovery. By the end, you will see how to apply these Tools to creating physical comedy and characters.

Our first few stops focus on the star of the tour—You.

As we progress through the Tour, we will expand the exercises to include group activities. This will offer deeper discovery opportunities with the Tools and their application. After all, performing, art, and comedy are group oriented. You usually do it for more than one person and not hidden in a closet by yourself.

The goal of any art form is to touch your audience. The audience needs to be changed in some way by your work. Sometimes the change is positive and sometimes the change is negative. But it rarely leaves the audience indifferent and untouched. What would be the point?

The Tour consists of different Tools. Please try all the Tools. Then pick and choose which ones work for you. Different Tools work at different times for different people. So you can take the Tour many times, and each time Discover a new meaning and a slightly different application for each Tool.

Explore, Challenge, and Choose what works for you.

First stop . . . SPACE.

Chapter 1

CREATING THE PERFORMING SPACE

Close your eyes. *Feel the Air Around You.* It is everywhere . . . between your toes, up your nose, under your armpit. In fact, you are not really sitting there—you are being buoyed in a sea of air.

Now just like a painter uses oil or watercolor or pastel or a sculptor uses clay or steel or metal, you will use *the Air Around You.* It is your medium.

Now focus on the air under your right armpit to your fingertips. The Air Pressure is going to be so great that it is going to push your arm up (1-1). YOU are not going to do anything. The Air Pressure is going to do it all. It is pushing your arm up until it reaches your shoulders. Then the Air Pressure on top of your arm will be so great that it will push your arm DOWN. You are Not Doing Anything. The Air is doing it.

Do this again with your other arm. Our hands become the paintbrushes. When you reach the top of your shoulders, the air

1-1 TUC! Up   **1-2 TUC! Down**

pressure at the top of your wrists will win and—TUC! (1-2)—
your hand floats down wrist first. When it hits the bottom and—
TUC!—up goes the wrist, and you are painting a beautiful wall
of Space.

FORM A CIRCLE

Make a circle. You are the Center of your Circle. Have everyone
be the same distance from the center of the circle (you) and the
same distance from each other. (Geometry 101: You are the center point of a circle and all the others are dots of equal distance
on the circumference of the circle. Note science and art meeting.)
Now stand with your heels together and toes pointing out. The
position is approximately ten minutes to two if you are not using
a digital clock, or it is a loose first position in ballet.

STRINGS

I'd like to introduce you to the String that grows out the top back crown of your head. Grab it and pull the end of it up and attach it to the sun (1-3). It is a lovely stretch along the back of your neck and down your spine.

BUNGEE CORDS

Please meet the Bungee Cords that are attached to the bottoms of your feet. Pull those Down and attach them with giant hooks to the center of the earth. You are now being pulled Down and Up at the same time. Look. Everyone has grown around the circle.

1-3   1-4

You are all filling Space. Now cut the cords and clip those strings and look around again. Everyone just shrank! (1-4).

PERFORMING SPACE

OK, connect those strings to the sun and those cords to the center of the earth and Eyeball, or more traditionally said, LOOK at the person in the Center of the Circle. If everyone is connected and focused, you have just built a giant Balloon or Bubble of Energy. If the person in the Center is not totally connected, you probably have made a donut of energy. Be sure to go for the giant balloon.

Congratulations. You have built a circle of SPACE. This is the Performing Space. It must be felt—especially if someone has paid hundreds of dollars for a ticket to see a performance. They want to see it and Feel it.

Chapter 2

FILL THE PERFORMING SPACE WITH ENERGY

Now take the Energy in the center of the earth and have it travel up your bungee cords through your feet, up your legs into your stomach, and up and through your right arm down to your hand and focus it out your pointing index finger. Say *ggHHEEE* as you shoot this laser beam of energy (by shaking your finger) at the person in the Center of the Circle. (If you don't wiggle and shake your finger, it's like a clogged pipe. You need to move your finger and get the energy flowing from your fingertip [2-1]).

If you are in the Center of the Circle, you will feel the energy tickling you. It helps a great deal, in fact it is essential, for the folks on the circumference of the circle to really look at you and focus the energy.

Yeah! You just made a SPACE filled with ENERGY and have now Energized yourself.

2-1

Do the other arm, and this time don't stop at one finger, add two, then three, then your hand and arm and your SHOOOOULDEEEERS, now your upper torso, then twist and shout and shake a leg(s) and jump up and down. (Now here comes the Fun part.) Scream and run around (only don't touch anyone or anything in space). Run up to people, but don't touch them because you know where you are in Space, and when the person in the Center of the Circle honks the POWERHORN.

(Oops! I forgot to tell you, if you are the one in the Center of the Circle, you get to hold the PowerHorn. What is a Power-Horn? Check out the horn that Harpo Marx uses or a hunting brass horn with a magnificent honk sound [2-2].)

And when you've had enough of these screaming maniacs, honk the horn ONCE.

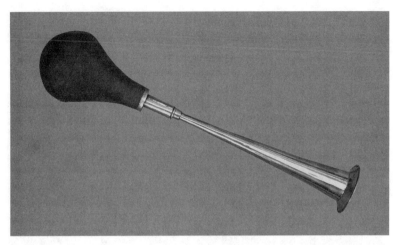

2-2

Here's the tricky part. You need to be multitasking, that is running around, screaming, not bumping into anything, and keeping a piece of your consciousness ready to hear the horn and stop on a dime at the first sound of it. If, for whatever reason, you miss the sound of the horn, you will be the only one running around screaming like a maniac with your proverbial pants down. So it really pays to multitask.

When you Stop or FREEZE, do you wiggle? No. Do you giggle? No. Do you talk? No. Do you Breathe? YES! Breathing is VERY IMPORTANT. If you don't, you are dead. And there is nothing worse than a dead performance.

TIME

Timing is everything. It is very important to know if your personal ticker (your sense of timing) is connected to the clock.

Here's how to tell. The person with the PowerHorn calls the amount of seconds and the start time. "From your freeze position, when you think seventeen seconds has passed, melt down to the ground starting NOW." Do not look at a clock or your watch. This is your personal clock ticking.

If you melted before seventeen seconds on the clock, time for you is fast. Your personal ticker is faster than the clock, and you probably feel like it takes forever for things to occur. If you melted after seventeen seconds on the clock, for you time moves slowly. You are probably more laid back. So if you are going to make the mark and time your moves for the director, camera, or joke, you need to know where your timer stands. If you are fast, then you might want to wait a few seconds from when your natural instinct to move occurs. If you are slower, then you need to move a few seconds earlier than you naturally feel it is time. This is helpful information in life. You can release some stress when you realize that everyone is not always late. And things, which seem to take sooooooo long, are not really taking that long. And if your ticker is slow, then you need to add some zest and realize you are just a tad more laid back than the world ticker, and that's why everyone seems to be moving so fast for no apparent reason. You can and need to develop your sense of timing to the clock. Why? Because *Timing is everything*.

FREEZE GAME

OK, we left off, before Time took over, with everyone in a Freeze. This is called the Freeze Game. Everyone must remain in his or her Freeze. The trick is to keep that Energy shooting out all parts of your body the whole time. As soon as you start losing the energy, we can't feel you anymore, and we want our money back. So we can develop our ability to pull the Energy from the center of the earth. And guess what? There is an unlimited amount of Energy.

Have you ever been on the set, Bunkie? Are you tired? Worn out? Do you just want to go home, Bunkie? And the director calls

2-3 Freeze

"Reset to do it yet again!" Well, Bunkie, just reach into the center of the earth and pull out that Energy, and you can go all night!!!

Now look around at the body shapes (2-3). Each body shape is actually a Character of some kind. The shape is either an animate or living character like an animal; or it is an inanimate object like a mineral. Groups of bodies form larger pictures and relationships. Go around the room and describe what each body shape is. What is its BodyTalk? Is this figure/shape a monster? Can it also be a shelf and a door handle? What is the feeling attached to this figure? Identify each person in the room as a character. Once that is done, name a location, and go through the entire group again telling a story: "Once upon a time there was a Monster who was chasing a Rabbit and then there was a Door Handle and there was a Monkey . . ."

It sometimes makes sense, and other times it doesn't. What is important is to develop your Eye for seeing shapes, characters, and relationships. Oh . . . and your memory for what each shape was in a sequence.

This Freeze Game takes a long time to do. And staying frozen is a skill that develops the more you do it. Keeping the story alive and the characters full of their Vivance is a skill. Your body will shake, you will want to move, talk, giggle, see the other shapes. But your job is to focus and keep pulling that energy from the center of the earth to keep your character alive and vibrant.

RANGE

Once the story is told, pick one person who has held his or her Freeze and not wiggled, giggled, or talked. Have this person, as his or her character, walk quickly around the room. As this person/character passes you, Melt Down flat into the earth on your back with your hands at your side. You are your favorite soup or ice cream melting into the earth. Stay melting into the earth for a few minutes. Then, at the sound of the PowerHorn honking, you will go from zero energy to full-throttle energy by having your string at the top of your head pull you up (it looks like opening a pop-up card), and you will have all the energy you had when that PowerHorn went off and you originally froze. The ability to go from nothing to everything is your muscle for RANGE. You can turn yourself totally on and completely off at will. Impressive.

Chapter 3

SHARE THE ENERGY

In a word, *ggHHEEE DONG!* is Energy sharing. Now let's share that energy and range of feelings.

Eyeball your partner. (In more traditional language, LOOK at your partner.) Connect with your eyeballs. You should be so connected with energy, eyeball to eyeball, that if the energy was visible, the connection would look like two long ropes or cords of energy connecting eyeballs.

Take your zero position. (Heels together, toes pointing out, strings attached to the sun, bungee cords attached to the center of the earth, and eyeballs looking at the center of the circle or your partner.) Now pull the energy from the center of the earth and bring it up through your legs to your stomach and then up through your arm. Make a circle with your arm as you say *ggHHEEE*, doing the sound and movement together. Build up speed, and while eyeballing your partner, throw the energy through your arm into your fingers and shoot it through your fingers at your partner. When you Let Go of the energy say, *DONG!*

3-1 ggHHEEE DONG!

Your partner then receives the energy by catching it like a football in the stomach and saying/responding/shouting *DONG!* She takes the energy from her stomach and puts it in her hand solely. Now the energy is isolated in the hand, and from there your partner makes circles with the energy and eyeballing you, throws it back to you (windup) saying *ggHHEEE* and (throw) *DONG!* Repeat several times. (See The Backflip!, ggHHEEE DONG!, pages 180–147.)

This is the basic ggHHEEE DONG! Be sure to Eyeball your partner (focus) and Receive the amount and intensity of energy your partner sends. If, for example, you send (give) your partner lots of energy, she needs to take (receives) lots of energy. If you send (give) lots of energy to your partner and she only takes (receives) a little amount of energy then she is not receiving what you gave her. And we all know that it is impolite not to receive a gift!

THE GIFT OF ART IS GIVING AND RECEIVING ENERGY

If you do not receive what is given, then the communication is blocked. The full emotional experience is not being felt or the person receiving is not fully receiving your communication. He is either not open to receiving the energy, or he is not seeing the amount of energy coming, or he is scared to receive it, or he wants to control the energy flow and transform the power point of the energy to his definition of how much energy to give and receive. Whew! That's how relationships are born.

ggHHEEE DONG! BODY PARTS

Here comes the fun part. Body Parts. Eyeball your partner. Throw the energy to him. He receives it in his stomach, and this time takes the energy and isolates it in his hand. Then he takes his hand and puts it on his head. Now the energy is in his head. He takes his shaking energized head and throws the energy from his head to your head, and you receive it in your head.

3-2 ggHHEEE DONG! Body Parts: Shoulder to Shoulder

Take your shaking head, and put your hand on your head; transfer the energy to your hand. Now the energy is isolated in your hand, and you pick any part of your body: Put your energized hand on that body part—like your leg. Then throw the energy from your shaking leg to your partner's leg. Your partner receives the energy by saying *DONG!* and shaking his leg. He keeps the game going by picking other body parts, and pretty soon you have a cartoon going of quick-paced shaking body parts.

Be sure to say *ggHHEEE DONG!* with each throw. The faster you do it, the more accurate your body parts are hit, the more variation and imagination you use in picking body parts, the funnier it is. So you can pinpoint your energy throws. You can also receive energy anywhere in your body in a myriad of variations of rhythm and intensity. (See The Backflip!, ggHHEEE DONG!, pages 180–147.)

ggHHEEE DONG! FEELINGS

Now let's throw Emotions or Feelings. Again Eyeball your partner (focus) and wind up with the phrase "ggHHEEE I feel (and throw) HAPPY." Your partner then receives HAPPY (like receiving DONG!) in the tummy. Then your partner sends back HAPPY to you. This is giving and receiving the same feeling.

Next do MAD. You give Mad, and your partner receives MAD.

Now you send HAPPY to your partner, and your partner receives Happy, only this time your partner transforms HAPPY to MAD and winds up MAD and sends Mad to you. You receive MAD and transform it into another feeling or emotion.

You and your partner are sharing feelings and reacting to the feelings sent with another feeling. You receive the information

3-3 "ggHHEEE I Feel Mad!"

your partner sent, and then you either join him in the feeling or you transform the feeling to a new one, which you send to him. You are having an emotional relationship with your partner.

This is exactly what happens in acting—or in life. One person sends feelings to another person. That person takes it in to some degree, and then she responds to it by sending back another feeling—either in harmony with the feeling the first person sent or she transforms it to her feeling. For the communication to happen, both parties have to focus, look, see, receive, and respond.

I bet you never knew communication skills were simply an arm's throw away!

Chapter 4

CHROMATIC EXPERIENCE

Chromatic is a word I use to describe levels of physical and emotional expression. I once did an exercise where you had to draw a chromatic color chart of your body. One end was black, and the other end was white, and all the colors and hues of the rainbow were in between. (This was like the science experiment where you dunk a piece of paper in a liquid, and it comes out all the colors of the rainbow.) Then you moved according to the Essence of the color. Dark red to light pink to white—it was very expressive.

I encountered this concept again with Ctibor Turba. His Chromatic Experience was in being able to move the body in increments up and down by jumping and then again laughing in increments from neutral to the abstraction of laughter back to neutral. So the ability to express both your body and feelings could be so pinpointed that you could go up and down a scale of physical and emotional expression at will. Hello . . . Did anyone say Hit your Mark over and over and over again!

Chromatic Movement and Feelings   **17**

CHROMATIC MOVEMENT

Start in zero position. Attach your strings to the sun and your bungee cords to the center of the earth and fill the space with energy. Now your feet are at ten minutes to two. Raise your right foot and hit the ball of the foot on the ground hard. (Remember to make a direct hit with the ball of your foot; if you miss and hit the side—either inside or outside—you are sickling your foot. YUCK. It is not called SICKling for nothing. You will hurt and weaken your foot if you are not hitting the bull's-eye—the bottom of your foot.) Once you hit the ball of your foot on the ground, push hard on the ball. Use your bungee cord attached to your foot to pull your foot down. As you push down on your foot, you get pulled up by your string at the top of your head. It is as if a giant puppet master is pulling your strings. You are not doing any thing. The String is doing it all.

Then, balance on your right foot (4-1). In the process of being pulled up and pulled down at the same time, your left foot rises and you end up on the balls of both feet (4-2). Your weight is evenly balanced on the balls of both feet. Be very conscious of where your weight is resting (on the ball of your right foot), and then consciously let the strings shift the weight to both feet, and then to the ball of your left foot. When the weight is transferred, let your right foot rest flat on the ground and hit the left ball of your foot (4-3). Using your strings and bungee cords, repeat the movement. Do this several times until you are comfortable shifting weight from one foot to the other.

Now here comes the fun. Begin to speed up the process as the strings transfer the weight from one foot to the other. Hit transfer flat, hit transfer flat. Using your string, you will suddenly find you are getting pulled off the ground or HOPPING from one foot to the other—getting off the ground without thinking about

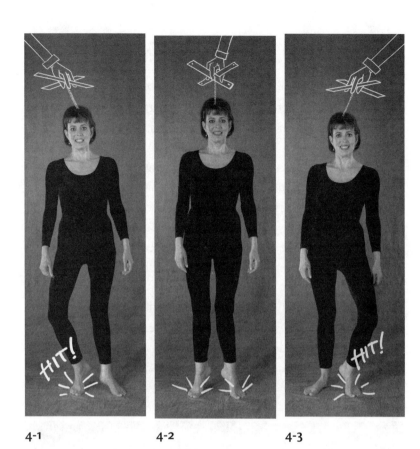

4-1   4-2   4-3

jumping. You are thinking of being pulled off the ground by your String. The result of thinking of being pulled when you are pushing is . . . you are flying.

Now get a rhythm going with your breathe by saying *shuuu, shuuu, shuuu* with each jump. Then add snapping your fingers to the rhythm. Gradually raise your knees higher in increments and jump faster until you reach a zenith, and then go down in the *same* increments you used going up. Keep incrementally going down until you are back to zero. Congratulations! You just did your first Chromatic Movement.

SHOOTING THE ENERGY

It is tricky coming down. Going up was easy, mindless fun. But hitting the same increments going down requires practice. The usual reaction is to hit the top and just crash-land at zero.

Once you hit zero, you aren't actually done. Congratulate yourself for getting to zero, and then SHOOT THE ENERGY into the center of the circle like a diver lying out after jumping off a diving board. One arm is straight in front of you, and one leg is straight in back of you. Both hands and toes are pointing the energy to shoot straight out like laser beams. If you let your hands relax and spread out your fingers, the energy is dissipated (4-4) and not as powerful as when your fingers are together and all pointing, focused, in the same direction (4-5).

Your leg needs to be straight and pointed. If it is not, then the energy is curved and is not as powerful as a direct hit. This particular game increases your ability to focus and direct the energy full throttle.

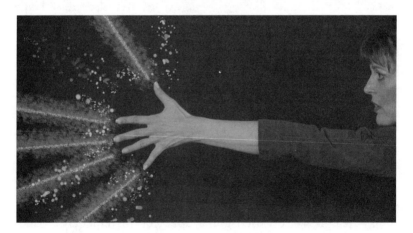

4-4

4-5

After SHOOTING THE ENERGY a few times, stop, take a big breath, and stretch your arms up, while your feet get pushed down—right side, left side, right side, left side. Then take a big breath and hold it (4-6), bend over (4-7), and touch the floor (4-8), if you can. If not, get as close as possible without hurting yourself. Point your right leg straight back (4-9), and press your left knee against your chest and blow the air out of your chest like a bellows (4-10). Go into a giant upside-down V (4-11)— rather reminiscent of Downward Dog for you yoga fans out there. Speaking of dogs, pretend you are a beagle and someone grabs you by the ears and pulls your head out as you bend your arms and curve your back (4-12). You are now a cobra snake as you raise your head, neck, and chest and finish it off by spitting *sss-saaaaaaaaaaaahhhh* into the center of the circle (4-13). Then go back to your inverted V, bringing your right foot to your chest, and blow the air out. Bend both feet and slowly, vertebra by vertebra, raise your body to a standing position. Head comes up last! Bring your arms up over your head in a full circle and down to your sides back into zero position.

4-6

4-7

4-8

4-9

4-10

4-11

4-12

4-13

Finding Your Funny Bone!

I salute you for doing the Salute to the Sun.

So we have experienced incremental Chromatic Movement with the JUMP. Great. You can apply this same concept to lots of movements, always being able to come down in the same increments you went up.

Staying in the Chromatic Experience, let's move on to CHROMATIC EMOTIONS.

CHROMATIC EMOTIONS: LAUGHING

What emotional expression is usually associated with comedy? LAUGHING.

Stand in zero position. You are *neutral*. (We'll discuss neutral in greater depth later.)

Now laugh a *tiny, tiny* laugh, then a *tiny* laugh, then a *small* laugh to a *big small* laugh, to a *medium* laugh, to a *big medium* laugh, to a *larger medium* laugh, to a *big* laugh, to a *great big* laugh, to a *really great big* laugh, to a *giant* laugh, to a *huge* laugh,

4-14

to the *extreme* of laughter, to the *abstraction* of laughter. Once you have hit the *abstraction* of laughter, work your way down to the *extreme*, then the *huge*, to the *giant*, to the *really great big* laugh, to a *great big* laugh, to a *big* laugh, to a *larger medium* laugh, to a *big medium* laugh, to a *medium* laugh, to a *big small* laugh, to a *small* laugh, to a *tiny* laugh, to a *tiny, tiny* laugh, to the *neutral/zero* position. Stay in zero position until everyone is done. WHEW! Laughing is serious business. (See The Flip!, Chromatic Emotions: Laughing, pages 147–180.)

Just standing in a line facing an audience or another person and laughing is tough. Then to incrementally—chromatically—go up the scale of laughter without pushing it, making it real, and coming back down can feel like nothing less than a miracle. The magic happens when you are really into laughing: The laughter flows, and you sail up and sail down. But this is where the gift of the moment meets the technique, and magic occurs.

I have seen a person do this one time, two times, and not get very far. Then all of a sudden something clicks, and that person goes nuts laughing, which of course affects the other people. Her energy hits the energy waves and—voilá—everyone is laughing.

Not pushing it or faking it can feel like a brick wall. It feels forced and can be enough to drive you to drama—but hang in there, 'cause if you can get to the abstraction of laughter, you have found your way to the ultimate dramatic moment.

What is the abstraction of laughter? Ever hear of the painter Edvard Munch? He painted a famous picture of a person on a bridge with his mouth wide open, body doubled up in what looks like a scream, but take that position, and you will see it is really the same body shape as a laugh—when you laugh so hard you cry. Ever hear of laughing yourself to death? Harlequin did. It's very old, but so true.

The ultimate comedy brings tears to your eyes. Laughing is the other side of crying. So if you can laugh, you can cry.

(These steps are listed to give you an idea of the increments. They are not written in stone. Basically, you go from no laugh to the tiniest indication of a laugh, or mere amusement, to the abstraction of laughter, or crying, in as many steps it takes to make a seamless transition.)

Experiment with other chromatic emotions and see where they take you. You are definitely going to want to do this exercise many times periodically. It is a real muscle stretcher.

So basically, we have experienced taking energy and moving it everywhere in our bodies. Then shooting it at (or giving it to) other performers' bodies and the audience. And in turn receiving (or taking) what they send back to us. We can play our bodies (oh, dear God . . . here it comes . . .) like an I-n-s-t-r-u-m-e-n-t. OK, OK, I said the I-word.

Now, we have the ability to incrementally adjust the energy in our bodies and our emotional expression with the Chromatic Movement and Chromatic Emotion. We can go from zero to full throttle and back to zero in any number of chromatic steps or all at once in a giant booster shot.

All we are missing in our bag of tricks is our POWER.

Chapter 5

THE POWER OF NEUTRAL

5-1

NEUTRAL + ZERO = POWER

What is neither happy nor sad but always ready and waiting to start?

Neutral.

Neutral in mask form can be called the neutral mask or the universal mask. I call it your POWERMASK because once you find your neutral point in your body, you have found your POWER, and you can go from + or – power or + or – characters at your will. Here is how to put your PowerMask in gear.

A PowerMask is made from either leather or white silicone. I am certain there are other materials that can create a PowerMask;

I just haven't personally experienced them. A PowerMask is smooth, with just the basics for features: forehead, eyes, nose, mouth, and chin. It is genderless and raceless. Although, some masks remind some people of male or female, Power knows no gender.

What exactly is Neutral? The essence of Neutral is to be just THERE in space. It is not happy or sad, it is just There. Like a car in neutral gear, it is turned on ready to go, but it goes nowhere because it makes NO JUDGMENTS. It OBSERVES everything it sees. And everything it sees is for the very first time. It forces you to REALLY SEE Everything. And, here's the challenge: Not To Judge It. You don't like it, you don't hate it, you don't fear it, you just see it. The Mask embraces the fact that what it is looking at exists. And then the Mask moves on to observing something else in its world.

This may sound really easy. Big deal—I just look at something. I've been looking at things all my life. Yes, you may have looked at many things all your life, but did you really see them? Really look? Really take the time to observe them, and just observe them, without making a judgment?

MASKS

A mask is magic. Masks are lovely works of visual art, but they do not come alive until you take your magic (energy) and blend it with the mask. You transform yourself into the mask, and the mask transforms itself into you. When you do this, a new entity is born—the character of the mask comes alive.

What makes a living mask? Look at your face in the mirror. Draw an imaginary line down the center of your face. The two sides of your face are not the same. Look at photo 5-2. What is the difference between the right side and the left side of his face?

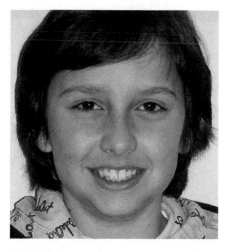

5-2

Can you See it? Look closely at the structure of his face.

Ah-ha! You got it! One of his eyes is bigger than the other eye. His face is asymmetrical.

If you look at your face in the mirror and draw an imaginary line down the center of your face, you will see that the two sides are not the same. Maybe one eyebrow is higher than the other, maybe one side of your mouth goes up and the other goes down, maybe your nose is crooked or even upside down! Either way, your face is not symmetrical. It is asymmetrical.

Let's take this a step further. Take a flashlight and hold it under your chin shining the light up. You look pretty scary or ghoulish. All your shadows are accented.

Now, take the flashlight and put it above your head shining down. You look angelic. You are highlighting your face. All the shadows disappear. (Remember this one, ladies, when you are searching for eternal youth.)

Now Smile. Be Happy. See how the highlight and shadow looks on your face.

Now Frown. Be Mad. See how the highlight and shadow changes.

So, to create feelings on your face, you need the play of light (highlight and shadow) on your facial structure. Your face's emotional expression comes from the imperfections in your facial structure and the play of light and shadow on your face.

Imperfection is really perfect—especially in comedy.

Body shape is really important in creating a character. It is essential in creating a comedy character (think Steve Martin, Jerry Lewis, Bill Irwin, Charlie Chaplin). The body shape creates the Walk and emotional Talk of your character.

CHARACTER MASKS

A character mask is a great way to discover the body shape and the essence of a character.

Let's look at the character mask, the Wolf.

5-3 Owl Mask

5-4 Tragedy/Comedy Mask

5-5 Wolf Mask

Turn away, with your back to the audience. Put on the mask. (Tip: Place the elastic strap high on the back of your head; it holds better.)

Now, on the beep of the horn, turn around and face the audience taking the body shape of the Wolf. Be sure to remember to be energized. We not only want to see a Wolf, we want to feel the Wolf. How does a Wolf stand? Some do it on all fours; others are the two-paw type. We will explore both.

The All-Fours Wolf is the traditional crawling style (5-6). How does a Wolf move? How does a Wolf move that is different from a dog? Be sure to keep your face UP, looking at the audience all the time.

5-6 All-Fours Wolf

If you put your face down, all we see is the top of your head. The character disappears, and we are left deciding on a new hairdo for you.

Also, keep the Face of the Mask Facing the audience. If you turn your back to us, all we see is your butt. I rest my case.

Now moving or crawling in the Wolf body shape, be a Happy Wolf.

Still moving or crawling in the Wolf body shape, be a Mad Wolf.

Great, and finally, still moving or crawling in the Wolf body shape, be a Sad Wolf.

The Sad Wolf is tricky

because to be sad your natural tendency is to look down. But in a mask, your head needs to stay Up looking at the audience, and your Body needs to go Down in sadness.

Emotional expression is not realistic in a mask. It is stylized. The emotions are real, but the feelings are expressed in a stylized fashion.

Great. Now it is time for the Two-Paw Wolf.

Stand up and face the curtain in the Wolf Mask. When the Horn honks turn around as a Standing Wolf.

Wait a minute! Wolves don't stand on Two Paws! That's right. There are other species of Wolves

5-7 **Standing-Up Wolf**

who stand on Two Paws. The Standing-Up Wolf is the wild-and-crazy-guy wolf (5-7).

So lift your head up. Put your arms out like a bodybuilder showing off his muscles. Share a few choice poses with us, and then walk toward us like the earth moves under your feet.

Be Happy, Mad, and Sad as this Wolf.

Now take the Mask off, and keep the Body Shape and Attitude of the Wolf.

Stanley Kowalski eat your manly heart out.

If you are having difficulty with the attitude of the Wolf or displaying a particular feeling, I have a very simple solution. BAG IT!

UTILITARIAN MASKS

A Paper Bag is a utilitarian mask. The utilitarian mask is made of a useful object. A Paper Bag is a pretty useful object, especially for showing and feeling emotions.

Do not use plastic bags for this exercise! You will drop dead. Remember: There is nothing worse than a dead performance!

The GIANT PAPER BAG Mask is Safe. It is FUN. And it is Guaranteed Success—even if you just put it on and only stand there.

I first discovered the Giant Paper Bag Mask with the Madcap Mimes in Maryland. One day, our company manager, Lana,

5-8 The Meeting of the Bags

brought these Giant Bags she discovered in front of a hardware store to our rehearsal. We played in them, and I haven't stopped playing since. The Giant Bags are the FINEST tool to use if someone has difficulty showing emotions. I used them at the Frostig Center in Pasadena for seven years with magical results.

The Big Bag Masks are larger than life. They require stylized movement. They are safe because you are completely covered except for your feet. All the audience sees are your feet. You make them come alive with your energy and big body movements. You hold the Big Bag from the inside to create a mouth. And you make the Bag come alive by blending your feelings with the Bag. Your techniques are shaking it, dancing in it, stop-action in it, and feet positions. It is a mask of REACTION. You have to Look and See what is going on around you, and then REACT to what is happening in a BIG Way.

Can we spell rhythm, timing, and CLOWNing?

THE MEETING OF THE BAGS

You will need Big Paper Bags Masks, which are available at my website: www.findingyourfunnybone.com. This piece can be done with any number of Happy Bags and Mad Bags.

Enter Happy Bag with three Happy Steps and Freezes.
Enter Mad Bag from the other side with three Mad Steps.
The Happy Bag Sees the Mad Bag and Jumps for Joy:
"Oh boy, someone to play with today!" (This line is not spoken. It is thought by the Mask.)
Freeze.
The Mad Bag sees the Happy Bag and is Mad: "Back off, I don't want to be with anyone today!"
Freeze.

The Happy Bag and the Mad Bag both face the audience at the same time. The Happy Bag is Happy and the Mad Bag is Mad.
Freeze.

Exit the Mad Bag, walking Mad behind the curtain.
The Happy Bag looks one way; then the Happy Bag looks the other way. The Happy Bag does an "Oh Well" move: "Oh well, I'll find someone else to play with today!" Exits, dancing off.

THE MEETING OF THE BAGS ON THE BENCH

Place three chairs or a long bench in front of the curtain. You will need one Happy Bag, one Mad Bag, and one Neutral Bag.

Enter the Neutral Bag. The Neutral Bag sits in the middle of the bench (feet together).

Enter the Happy Bag. Happy Bag Sees the Neutral Bag and jumps for Joy: "Oh Boy, someone to talk to on the Bench!" Happy Bag sits down next to the Neutral Bag. Happy Bag sits with Happy Feet (kick feet forward and back).

Enter the Mad Bag. Mad Bag Sees the Neutral and Happy Bags on the Bench. Mad Bag is furious: "Someone on my Bench!" The Mad Bag gets an idea. The Mad Bag flops onto the bench (sits with his legs and feet spread as wide as possible).

The Neutral Bag does nothing.

The Happy Bag Sees the Mad Bag and jumps for joy. And then the Happy Bag sits down.

The Mad Bag Sees the Happy Bag. The Mad Bag jumps up and is Mad.

5-9 The Meeting of the Bags on the Bench

The Neutral Bag sits there doing nothing.

The Mad Bag sits down with Feet Wide Apart.
The Happy Bag starts to rub against the Neutral Bag (like a cat).
The Mad Bag starts to bang against the Neutral Bag.
The Happy and Mad Bag build their rhythm, both banging and rubbing against the Neutral Bag.
Suddenly the Neutral Bag surprises the Happy Bag and the Mad Bag and gets up and walks off.
The Mad Bag and Happy Bag fall into each other.

The Mad Bag jumps up. Exit the Mad Bag in a huff.
The Happy Bag stands up. Looks one way. Looks the other way. Does an "Oh Well" shrug to the audience and lies down on the entire bench.

These Bag pieces are fun and can be played many, many times, allowing everyone to experience the feelings of Happy, Mad, and Neutral. Oh, but wait a minute—we haven't explored what Neutral really is.

All right, enough of this safe stuff. It is time to take the Big Bag off, drop your Character Masks, and BE your most POWER-FUL SELF. It is time to discover the essence of the PowerMask, the starting point of your Power—your Zero or Neutral point in your body.

You will need one PowerMask, an outside observer or observers, and a full-length mirror. The observers' job is to mirror to you how you are moving, when you are in your neutral point and when you are out of your neutral point.

The mirror is optional. This exercise can be done with a mirror or without a mirror. Each version offers a different experience in the mask. Each experience is valid, and all these experiences lead to the discovery of your most powerful self.

Without the mirror: Look at the mask. Touch it, feel it, study it. Put it on. Let your body adjust itself to how it feels best in the mask. Once you have blended yourself with the mask, slowly turn around and look at the audience.

With the mirror: Look at the mask. Touch it, feel it, study it. Put the mask on in front of the mirror. Take a moment, or six, and look at yourself in the mask in the mirror. Let your body adjust itself to how it feels best in the mask. Once you have adjusted yourself with the mask, slowly turn around and look at the audience.

(It is a good idea to wear all black or all one color—no stripes or plaids or floral prints because they distract from the mask.)

A PowerMask requires a very specific body posture. You have to be neutral in your body for the PowerMask to come alive. Your weight is evenly balanced on both feet, which are shoulder-width apart. The feet are parallel. The hips are facing evenly to the front. Both shoulders are even and relaxed. The head is resting evenly between the shoulders with your chin down and the crown of the head up. Arms are relaxed, and hands are resting on the thighs. You are relaxed. Your body shows no signs of tension, and you don't feel any tension either.

Hmmm, what position does this resemble? Yes, folks, Neutral in the Mask is really Zero Position without the Mask. So Neutral is Zero.

Try it. Discover it for yourself. It is the only way to own it.

NOTHING IS EVERYTHING

Neutral and Zero are not nothing. They are everything. Because once you have discovered for yourself your neutral, you can fill the space in your body and then keep moving outward, filling any space you need to with energy, but not judgment.

This is pure power. You play an arena, no problem. You play a small stage or to the tiny camera lens—no problem. You can adjust your space and energy to meet the specific situation.

Art is an exchange of energy.

Your Power is being able to feel the energy in All of yourself, and then filling the space you are in with that energy. You have to be able to fill your space—big like an arena, small like a stage, and tiny like a camera. So, if you know your point of Power, of being in Zero Position and Neutral, you can bump it up or bring it down according to the needs of the situation.

When you feel all that energy, the audience feels all that energy. You want people to feel you whether you are on-screen or live. Remember what makes Art with the capital A is the exchange of energy and the audience feeling you. So you need to be able to feel ALL of yourself for the audience to feel you.

What's the old saying: You have to love yourself before you

are open to someone else loving you. Here's how to find that Love.

OK, you are standing in front of the mirror, blending with the mask; you have turned and adjusted your body to be in the perfect neutral.

You see, the Mask will not let you lie. If you are not totally in neutral, that unneutral part of your body will scream at the audience with judgment. It becomes very clear where you are holding onto imaginary helpers with your hands, or desiring to defend yourself from imaginary foes in your feet and shoulders, or your head is screwed on funny and you protect yourself with your head. It all hangs out very clearly. But once you kick into neutral—and you feel and see the power of neutral, no judgment—you own whatever environment you are performing in, big, small, or tiny. You want to be noticed—go into neutral and people unconsciously need to look at you because your body is demanding it by the power it is radiating and the space it is taking and filling.

Neutral is passion waiting to explode in your face.

NEUTRAL AT THE BEACH

Staying in your Neutral, begin to walk. Walking in neutral is different from your normal walk. It is slower. Look at the room you are in and also at the people in the room. Really look at them for the very first time. You have never seen them before.

Time to be born Neutral!

Now you are on a beach. Walk on the beach and look at everything for the very first time. I repeat, for the very first time. Really see the sky and the sand and the water. Are there clouds floating by or is this a beautiful sunny beach without a cloud? Is the sand warm or cold? (You see, you want to see vividly, but you don't want to judge what you see. If you like warm beaches or cold sand, this is irrelevant information in neutral. These are just facts. It is warm. It is cold.)

Now see a stone on the ground at your feet. Look at it. Bend over and pick up the stone. Look at it. Then look at the ocean in front of you. HURL the stone into the water. Watch it land in the water. Then sit in neutral on the sand and watch the spot in the water where the stone landed.

This seems simple enough: Pick up a stone and throw it. Do not be deceived by the simplicity of the action. It is far from simple.

See the stone.

Observe the stone.

Bend to pick up the stone—in neutral.

Hold the stone.

Feel the stone.

See the water.

Think of the idea of throwing the stone.

Wind up.

HURL it.

Watch it fly.

Watch it splash the water.

Watch it disappear.

Sit down on the sand in Neutral.

Watch the spot where it used to be in Neutral.

Do all this and do not tell a story by adding feeling or relationship. It's sort of like a police report of an event. Only the facts are relevant—no feelings. But facts that are full of life and energy.

Also, I keep capitalizing the word HURL. HURLING a stone is throwing it as far and as hard as you can with all your might and force—or directly focused energy. It is the extreme of ggHHEEE DONG!

After you complete putting on the PowerMask for the first time. Ask yourself how you felt. It evokes a myriad of emotions. All are valid.

Some people say they can't breath, others feel weird, some feel freed or liberated. A few have never felt like this before. They are all experiencing a part of themselves that they probably never consciously connected with—their Power.

It is important to honor whatever experience the person had. It is also important to keep asking questions to pinpoint exactly the experience the person had. For example, weird is too general a description. How was it weird? How was it different from how you usually feel? Being specific in description and knowing what emotional label goes on what you feel is a very important skill to have whether you are acting, clowning, or living a normal life.

Stand up, turn around, and take the PowerMask off. Turn, face the audience, and tell us how you felt.

Then turn away from the audience, and without putting the PowerMask on, go into Neutral. Repeat the first walk on the beach and especially the HURLING of the stone section. When you can do this with the same force without the mask, you have found your Power.

From here you can do anything. Which is exactly why finding your Zero + Neutral = Power is so important. It gives you a powerful, energized, nonjudgmental starting point from which you can create vibrant characters that will touch the audience. Nothing, Being There in Space, is everything—especially in Comedy.

What does Neutral have to do with comedy? It's where it starts.

Next stop is Silence.

Chapter 6

THE ART OF MIME

Some of the greatest come-
dians never said a word—
for either their whole careers
or most of them. I am talking about the silent film
stars: Chaplin, Keaton, Lloyd.
They were the Kings of
Comedy in their day and
still are. Why? Because their
bodies did the talking.
Their medium was their
bodies and the air around
them. Their medium was
based on the Art of Mime.

6-1 Claude Kipnis

Mime is an art form
that uses your body and the air around you to create illusions or
make-believe. With mime, you can make anything from nothing.

All you need is your body, imagination, and the air around you. There are no limits.

And when you are clowning, you will explore the outer limits.

So it is an essential part of comedy.

To do mime, you have to believe what you are doing. If you don't believe what you are doing, no one else is going to—kinda like life, eh?

THE WALL

See a wall in front of you. Feel the wall in front of you (6-2). What color is it? Really look at it and see. Is it red, green purple, rainbow, translucent? Now what does it feel like? What is it made of? Is it bricks, roses, mud, vinyl, CD covers? What does it smell like? Is it dirt, roses, cinnamon, chocolate?

My wall is usually red brick, and it smells like hot fudge. Everyone's wall is different.

So, mime is like a coloring book. It gives you the outline, and you as the performer, or you as the audience, get to see whatever details you like. Which is why mime is so magical. It is personal to each of us. We see the details we want to see.

As the performer, you must experience the wall with all your senses in order to really create it. You have to believe it is there. If you believe it, we will believe it. However, you need to pick exactly the symbol we can relate to. The key is to use the *detail* of the object so that we know instantly, exactly, what we are looking at. But I am going too quickly. Let's make our first wall.

OK, Hands UP!

SMASH your hands against the wall.

Keep them there.

6-2

It is easy to grab something. It is hard to remember to LET
GO! But LETTING GO is what creates the illusion of the WALL.

OK, now let go like a hot potato. Smash your hands on the
wall making a smashing sound, hold for a second, and take them
off—like they are burning with the sound that goes with it.

Your hands are now holding two big juicy grapefruits. Pick
them up and SMASH them against the wall. As they are dripping
and oozing, your grapefruits turn into pancakes. Grapefruit, to
pancake, pancake to grapefruit, grapefruit to pancake. Make the
sounds. The sounds are like your inner dialogue. It is the music
in your ear that gives you a rhythm to work with. It is important
to have this musical sound or dialogue in your mind. So don't
sensor it if it just starts happening. Keep doing this; only this
time think the sounds.

Now we are going to walk our hands on the wall. Just like in life, you put one foot in front of the other as you walk. Do the same thing with your hands on the wall. Only there is one catch—literally.

Take your right hand away from the wall, and leave your left hand fixed, stuck on the wall. That is called Fixed Point. Your left hand is stuck or fixed to the wall, and your body can move in any direction—forward, backward, up or down, side to side. Your hand remains fixed to the wall at that point. Now release your left hand and repeat the fixed point with your right hand. You are grabbing the wall and letting go of it. You are getting stuck and unstuck. Pushing the air, compressing it, until it becomes a wall and then releasing it.

Both hands hit the wall—grapefruit to pancake, pancake to grapefruit. Then with one hand—grapefruit to pancake, pancake to grapefruit. Now walking your hands, making the sounds, seeing the wall, feeling the wall, smelling the wall, grabbing it, letting go of it, pushing it, releasing it. It is time to grab the tiny handle sticking out of the wall, turn it, open the tiny door, see the audience, wave, close the window-door, grab the outside edges of your wall, pick the wall up and throw it away to your right—careful not to hit anyone else with your wall.

Congratulations! You have just built your first mime illusion, the wall!

LEAVE AND GRAB

Shhhhhh. I have a secret to tell you. What is the difference between a beginner wall and an advanced wall? A beginner will gently and gingerly place his hands on the wall. It is enough to see it and believe there is a wall there. The advanced mime will SMASH her hands on the wall and really push on it with all her might, which creates a very clean and definite wall.

Try this. Place your hands flat on the floor and push. Note that your wrists are at a 45-degree angle or perpendicular to the floor. Your fingers and palms are pushing equally on the floor. Now do that to the air. Your wall will definitely graduate from beginner wall to advanced WALL.

So, to do a great mime wall it is not enough to just do the technique of placing your hands on the imaginary wall: you really need to go for the gusto of a definite and forceful pressure. Basically, the excellent wall is not half-baked. It is created with your fullest intension. You believe and act on it with 110 percent conviction and body expression.

This technique is called Leave and Grab and can be applied to any object you wish to create. So it is the basis of a world you can create with your body and the air around you.

Welcome to your new World.

CREATE A MIME PIECE

Using the technique of Leave and Grab, create an object. Then use it, so we know exactly what that object is immediately.

Make a story using an object that has a beginning, middle, and an end with a character other than yourself. The events in the story take form because of the emotional reactions of the character to the events.

In other words, the emotional choices you make dictate the type of reaction to the event. For example, your character is playing catch with a ball. The ball hits the character in the face. He can laugh, cry, faint, be in shock, be embarrassed, and so on. His next physical reaction depends on this choice. If he chooses to laugh, he might grab the ball and play with it before he tosses it back. If he cries, he might beat up the ball and shake his fist at the other character in rage before he violently throws the ball back in an attempt at revenge.

So emotional expression leads to relationship . . . ain't that the truth.

Another aspect of mime, which is also essential to comedy, is that the audience is a vital part of the equation. Let's face it. Mime needs an audience. You rarely do it in the closet. (Although many do it in a box—sorry, I couldn't help it.) You need other people to see it.

Comedy is like that, too. You need the audience to see what you are doing. And you need to include them in everything you do. So, being conscious of staging is an important element of mime, which is also helpful in comedy. Most mime illusions are best seen from the front. Arena-style seating is tough for mime illusion. Also, often the mime partners with the audience to express his or her feelings and shares them with the audience. The same happens with comedy. The "take" to the audience is an art form (Jack Benny, Jackie Gleason, Carol Burnett). The "double take" is in the same category.

When you are making an object for people to see, it is most powerful in a direct line to the audience. So put your refrigerators, cabinets, tables, and walls facing the audience. This also enables them to see your face and physical reactions so they can immediately share what you are experiencing.

You accidentally lay your hand on a hot stove.

The stove is positioned between you and the audience.

You put your hand on the stove.

You feel the heat.

You react by pulling your hand off the stove.

You have a moment of shock.

You look at your hand.

You see the burn.

Your mind registers pain.

Your body registers the pain.

You scream—body and mouth.

You jump up and down in pain.

You roll on the floor writhing.

You sit up, lick your hand, wave it, kiss it.

Etc.

If you were facing the side, we'd miss most of the reaction facially and some of the physical reaction.

When you are clowning, the audience is your partner. You share with them—because sharing is good—but that's the next step. The In-Your-Face Art Form—the Clown.

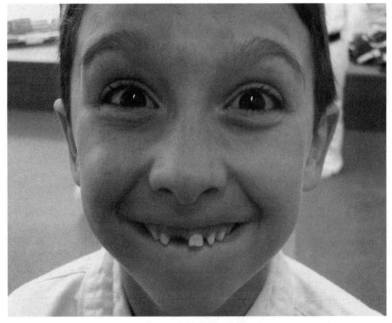

6-3

Chapter 7

THE CLOWN

WHAT IS A CLOWN?

"A Clown is someone who 'finds their stupid and stays in it.'"

—Pierre Byland

"A Clown's job is to remind you of your humanity."

—Ctibor Turba

7-1

Whew! This is no joke. Clowning is a serious business. And comedy is too.

Real feelings and reactions are funny. Trying to be funny and/or "showing" feelings are formulas for a flop.

So, just like in drama, you need to experience the angst. Angst is King in comedy.

All those feelings that are considered negative feelings in our society—such as fear, nervousness, hyperactive, distracted, worried, anxious—are golden in comedy. Have you ever been told you are too sensitive? Has anyone ever said you are so dramatic? Are you hyperactive? Overemotional? Easily distracted? YES!!! GREAT!!! These are the emotions you want to tap into. Whale and wail in.

But how?

Say hello to that little (and not so little) voice in your head that tells you, "You are so stupid and what a dumb thing you did and how could you do THAT." Give it $100 and tell it to go to San Francisco—have a cup of coffee, lunch, cocoa, whatever—but to leave you alone for a couple of hours. If it is an avid negotiator, give it whatever it demands to take a powder so you are freed up to do and say the first thing that comes into your mind.

Now.

Take a clown nose and place it in your right hand.

Take your zero position.

All right.

Ready.

March.

THE MILITARY CLOWNS

7-2 Head UP!

Ten Hup!
About Face (face the audience).
HEAD UP.
SHOULDERS UP.
CHEST OUT.
TUMMY IN.
BOTTOM OUT.
KNEES BENT.
TOES IN.
Hold that Shape.
PREPARE NOSES.
(Raise both hands to nose level.)
NOSES ON.
(Place the clown nose on nose.)
PREPARE TO MARCH OOOOOEEEEE.
(March in a specific rhythm in place.)

MARCH OOOOOEEEEEE.

(March three steps forward saying ooooeee, ooooeee, oooeeee with each step.)

STOP.

LOOK AT AUDIENCE.

RUB HANDS AND SAY,

"OOOOEEEEE, OOOOEEEEE, OOOOOEEEEE."

LOOK AT AUDIENCE.

SHAKE YOUR FINGER AT EACH AUDIENCE MEMBER SAYING: "NO NO NO NO NO NO."

STOP.

LOOK AT THE AUDIENCE.

BECOME TERRIFIED.

DO A CLOWN SCREAM.

RUN OFF, STAYING IN THIS BODY SHAPE.

Congratulations! You just made your first clown!

7-3 No! No! No!

THE NOSE

A clown nose is one of the smallest masks you can wear.

It is the button, so to speak, that allows you to change your body shape into however your clown stands. Once you put it on, it's like pushing the button. Take a moment (or two or three), and let your body reshape. Just like in the character mask, once you have found that shape, stay in it. Walk, run, look, see.

Now here's where you begin to add onto the neutral. In this new body shape, you will Feel, you will experience all your emotions, only they will be expressed through this new body shape. So you are happy, sad, angry, joyful in a new form. Your VOICE will also change. It will be different from you normal speaking voice. Play with it until you find the sound that is your clown's sound.

The body shape we took in Military Clowns is just one of a gazillion shapes you might take. It is here only to say hello to your body, to experience another shape. Find your own new shape. And enjoy it.

We are now ready to meet your clown.

THE CLOWN INTERVIEW

You will need a curtain that is about one foot off the floor. The idea is to see your feet and legs up to around midcalf, so twelve inches usually is good. I use two buckets with a pole, hang a shortened curtain, and voilá. It needs to be sturdy enough to take abuse and flexible enough not to hurt anyone if it falls. More about THE CURTAIN later.

Clown noses are a must. I like the soft, foam-ball noses that require double-stick tape to really keep on. They offer lots of comedy when they fall off. They also come in a wide range of colors and sizes. Picking your nose never was so exciting. Those are the props. Here is what you do.

FEAR is a major factor in comedy. Real, true fear works wonders to bring real chuckles to your audience. It is the Mother of Comic Invention.

Pick your nose. (You can pick your nose. You can pick your friends. You can't pick your friend's nose.)

Go behind the curtain and double stick your clown nose onto your nose.

7-4

Take a moment to blend your magic with the nose and transform yourself into your clown shape.

You are going to have to open the curtain and enter the stage.

You are TERRIFIED to go out there.

As you peek out, see the audience and be very frightened of them (7-4).

Play with the curtain. Use the curtain in a million and one ways to get out in front of it (7-5).

7-5

The Clown   53

Once you have crossed the curtain line and made it out onto the open stage, you are completely in your clown.

See the audience and be thrilled to your tippy toes to be onstage with the whole audience to play with.

Oops. You will also need someone to interview you. The Interviewer will ask these classic Ctibor Turba questions.

Interviewer: "Hello. What's your name?"

Clown: Using your new clown's sound say the VERY FIRST THING THAT POPS INTO YOUR HEAD.

There is no wrong answer.

Remember, the odds are, you have more than one clown living inside you. So what clown appears today may not be the one who appears the next time or the next time. It can take a while before you find the dominant clown, so to speak.

So go with the flow. Remember, that voice in your head is having coffee down the street so nobody cares what you say—take a ride on the wild side. Logic is out the window. Good Taste took a powder. It's You and Spontaneity alone at last. Ahhhhhhh.

Maybe your name is Sydney, or Pickles, or George, or I-Don't-Know. They all work just fine.

Interviewer: "Where did you come from?"

Clown: "Over there. The Moon, Paris, my Mommy, a 1947 Chevrolet, the outside fungus on blue cheese."

Interviewer: "Show us how you got here."

Clown: (It's Show and Tell Time. Can it get any better than this?) Show or mime how you got here.

Interviewer: "We are looking for a model clown. Please hit the runway with your model clown walk." (Humming or singing just the melody of "A Pretty Girl Is Like a Melody" adds a nice touch and helps the clown move more freely.)

Clown: Struts his or her stuff down the runway.

CLOWN TRICK

Interviewer: "We are looking for a tricky clown. I understand you have a famous (clown's name) Clown Trick. May we see it now?"

Clown: Does a TRICK.

STOP!
What is a Clown Trick?
In short, a Clown Trick is absolutely anything.
Be sure to follow it up with a TAH DAH!
You know TAH DAH—where you raise your arms and shout TAH DAH!!!

7-6 TAH DAH!!!

And you are happy and proud to your tippy toes about what you did.

In long form, a clown trick is any skill you have: juggling, dancing, acrobatics, singing, mime, balancing, playing an instrument. All clown tricks, whether in the long or short form, are followed by the joyfully proud TAH DAH!!!

Have any of you ever seen the *David Letterman Show*? Do you remember the Stupid Human Trick segments? Those are clown tricks—the good, the bad, and the ugly, and all definitely funny.

So your clown does a Trick.

THE INTERVIEW CONTINUED

Interviewer: "We are looking for a song and dance clown. I'd like to see your famous (clown name's) song and dance."

Clown: Sing and dance as your clown does. Do an original song and dance or rely on some old favorites like "Twinkle Twinkle Little Star," the ABC's, "I Wish I Were an Oscar Meyer Weiner," or the latest pop song or an original that is debuting right now.

Interviewer: "What is special about you? Why should I hire you over the other clowns?"

Clown: Say the first thing that pops into your head. Remember, Logic and Good Taste are gone. You may say something profound. You may say something stupid. There is no wrong answer. My nose is Blue. I am funny. I am stupid. I like to swim every day at 4 p.m. precisely. I work for world peace.

Interviewer: "What would you like to be paid?"

Clown: Does your clown work for peanuts literally or the big bucks, francs, pesos, or candy. Or are you free?

Interviewer: "Great. It was nice meeting you. Thanks for stopping by. We'll see you later."

Clown: Exits through the curtain.

ENTRANCES AND EXITS

Crossing the dividing line that is the Curtain is no small feat. In fact it is an art form in itself. You have heard of the phrase "Making an Entrance" or "Making an Exit"? This is your first and last impression on the audience and you want to make it memorable.

So how do you do that?

STOP!

Yes, that's right. To Start, you need to STOP! If that isn't Clown logic, I don't know what else is.

You will need:

A Curtain

A Tambourine

An Audience

Now go behind the Curtain and take a strong body shape: may be your Clown shape, may be a Monster. Pick an emotion: Happy, Mad, or Sad.

The person with the Tambourine will beat out an increasing rhythm, a crescendo.

When the Tambourine reaches the height of the crescendo, you BURST through the Curtain in your character's body shape, filled with the emotion you chose.

Let's say you picked Happy. You POP out from behind the curtain Happy and STOP!

Give the Audience a "Freeze Frame Moment." You stand Looking at them in a strong body shape. You are fully energized and shooting the energy at the audience, so they FEEL your Entrance (7-7).

Now run for a few steps down to the edge of the stage area and STOP. LOOK each person in the audience in the Eye being Happy.

7-7 The STOP!

The trick is to be Happy in a different way for each person you Look at.

You are exploring the many ways you express Happy. Some times you are Happy in a big way, other times you are Happy very subtly. But no two Happy Looks are identical.

This is Chromatic Emotional Expression—out of order.

Meanwhile, the Tambourine is beating out an ever-increasing beat. You are always looking directly into the Eyes of each audience member. (Remember: Clowning is the In-Your-Face Art Form.)

Once you have Given the Audience your Feeling (ggHHEEE DONG! each audience member through your eyes), turn.

Run upstage to the Curtain and STOP!

Turn again.

Face the Audience.

Give them a final "Freeze Frame Moment" of Happy.

And then Exit.

Be sure to close the Curtain behind you.

The Stop! or Arrêté, as it is called by many teachers and performers, can be done with two or more performers. This variation develops rapid relationships between the performers and the audience with clear, specific action and reactions. When played in full force, it is very funny and cartoonlike. It also is invaluable in creating vibrant funny characters with spontaneous, creative reactions.

The ability to pause and look directly at the audience took Jack Benny very far. He was renowned for his Look. The Stop! allows the audience to really see and feel your character.

REMEMBER: *Your Exit Is as Important as Your Entrance.*

This is your final moment where so much can happen unexpectedly.

Chapter 8

THE CURTAIN . . .
THE DIVIDING LINE TO THE
GIFT OF THE UNEXPECTED

This cloth is the dividing line between you and the audience. It is the on and off switch for the lights. It is the difference between Reality and the Clown's Real World. Reality lives behind the curtain. Spontaneity, illogical logic, play, extreme emotions, revenge and rewards, giving and receiving, sharing with the audience— all live in front of the curtain. To cross the great divide takes a great deal of courage. You need to drop everything and let it all hang out, so to speak. The curtain can be your friend. It provides you a safe haven to get off the stage, hide, dress, play, amuse the audience and yourself. It is the magic line that separates the co-median, performer, entertainer, and actor from the audience.

It is the beginning and it is the end.

Ctibor Turba introduced me to this particular curtain. It is slightly askew because it is too short to really cover you completely.

8-1

So you are vulnerable from the moment you walk behind it. It is an illusion of protection. And just like in comedy—and life—it is perfect in it's imperfection. Because it is too short, not complete, and off makes it the perfect vehicle for comedy.

The challenge was constructing a Portable Curtain that

- would cover both large and small;

- is flexible enough to take great abuse, while the clowns explore their fears and overcome them;

- is easy, but not too easy, to rebuild on the spot if it fell; and

- would signal to the audience The End.

Luckily, Lol Levy is a very inventive person, and he created the two-bucket, white, PVC-pipe curtain design that works—

especially when it doesn't (8-1). As one clown student said to me, "It rocks!" The interview or the entrée is not over until all clowns have exited and the curtain is closed.

The curtain is closed—such a simple phrase, such a simple concept. And yet sometimes, so difficult and funny to do. This can be a tricky business, especially if your clowns are frisky and the curtain gets pulled down or falls. The scene is not over until the curtain is closed properly: This can be a magnificent comedy gift.

TIS A PITY IF THE GIFT IS MISSED

When you least expect it—*It* happens. The Unexpected visits you and hands you a Gift. You have to be aware to see it and receive it and conscious enough to immediately share it with your partner—the audience.

The Gift is the moment when something happens that you did not expect. It is the Gift of the Unexpected: the curtain falls, a prop gets stuck, a line is forgotten, a baby cries, the phone rings, a fire truck goes by, a cell phone rings, people enter late, your contact lens leaps out of your eye just as you are reaching the emotional climax of your speech, a prop sticks, the light fixture falls. You get the gist. It happens in the moment, and if you had tried to plan it, it probably wouldn't have happened as well as it just spontaneously did. And when it does, you need to be ready to use it or improvise off it, and then go back to the line of action that was occurring before the Gift. Robin Williams is great at this. The *Carol Burnett Show* is full of them.

Ctibor Turba would say "Tis a pity"—if a golden moment occurred and you did not receive it and use it. The pity was that you missed the opportunity to create another moment of comedy.

You need to be conscious of everything around you. Multitasking is not just a corporate concept. It is a way of life for comedy. What you are doing, what the other performers onstage are doing, the lighting, the music, the sound, and the audience— being so tuned in and yet appearing to be so tuned out— is the delicate balance you need to achieve. The more you do it, the more obvious it becomes when it happens, and also your ability to go with it increases.

The other challenge is in knowing just how long to play the gift. Too long, and you have disrupted the flow of the action. Too short, and we don't understand what you are doing or worse we think—OOPS—somebody really screwed up.

One way to practice this very important skill is with the Curtain. My bucket/pole curtain is purposely constructed not to be extremely sturdy. A good pull of the curtain or a swift kick of the bucket will send the curtain rod out of joint, and the curtain will fall. Remember, the scene is not over until the curtain is closed. So if you add the element of time—anxious, anxiety-driven, pressurized time of "Hurry Up"—you create a desperate need to get the curtain fixed and closed. The anxiety of getting the curtain back is a terrific setup for fun and funny.

AN EXAMPLE OF A GIFT

I had a group of students doing their own entrées. (An entrée is a clown skit; see Chapter 17, "The Clown Entrée.") They were exhausted from a rehearsal for their upcoming show, and the entrées were very lackluster and not really up to snuff. Basically, they just wanted to end class and go to lunch. Just as the last group was finishing, they closed the curtain, and it fell to the ground. The students wanted me to call it and end the scene. But a key to comedy is having a problem and a deep need to fix it. Oh, how they wanted to leave—but the situation was perfect. All the elements were there for a real entrée.

Putting up the curtain is really a two-person job. The clown who accidentally toppled the curtain was attempting to do it, and it kept falling. And the more her clown tried to fix it, the worse it became. Finally, I sent in a second clown who tried but wasn't getting anywhere. The question did arise, "How many clowns does it take to put up a curtain?"

And so I sent in a third clown, who decided he was the Curtain Police and his job was to see that the curtain was put up immediately. I now had the three basic clown characters for an entrée: the Auguste, the White Face Clown, and the Ringmaster. (See Chapter 17 for more about these three key characters.) The Auguste (Clown 1) was rolling headfirst into the buckets with her butt waving at us, and the White Face Clown (Clown 2) was arguing with the Curtain Police (Ringmaster) on how to get the curtain up and who would do it. After many attempts, the job was done, and a true entrée had occurred.

There was NEED, passion, strong characters, and free spontaneous improvisation that came from what was actually happening onstage. In the moment, a real entrée was born from the situation, with relationship and real emotions and events and feelings that occurred because of what was happening onstage and what had spontaneously happened. It was truly a Gift.

BACK TO THE INTERVIEW

Whew! You did it. We have met a part of you, you may not have known existed. We may never meet this clown again, or we may now begin to develop this clown.

Depending on who is in the audience, it can be very helpful to have the audience/class members take a moment to write a few descriptive words about what they saw. The clowns do not get to read them until everyone has been interviewed. These are anonymous observations. These adjectives and descriptions are to give you some perspective on who your clown is.

Maybe one paper you read describes your clown as a shy, funny, timid, aggressive, and verbal clown. While another person saw your clown as a manipulative, sexy, brassy, trying too hard, flighty clown with great dance moves who loves banana pizza and who revels in hiding things and being mysterious. Whatever. Each person's Eye gives you a view of exactly who your clown is.

You may be very surprised by this and discover things about yourself you never expected, and more important, things you never expected to share with others. Is your clown really obnoxious and belligerent while in normal life you are quiet and reserved? I often see this happen. The clown is the opposite of the person who is taking the class.

Once I had a painfully shy girl do the interview. I was thrilled she was even willing to give it a go. I had her do it with a group of people so she would feel safer to let her clown make an appearance. Well, the Nose is a button, and boy did hers get pushed. She became so aggressive and abusive she began beating up the other clown. I was really torn whether to stop her or let her continue. I did not want to stifle this great release, but I also did not want anyone to be heading to the hospital. And in the group of clowns onstage with her was another clown who in normal life was a very aggressive and eager participant. His clown was very shy and timid. So the Timid became the Bruiser and the Bruiser became the Timid. They traded places, as each experienced another aspect of him- and herself.

You may have many clowns living inside you just waiting to make an appearance. Or perhaps, you meet one clown, and the next time another one shows up, and the third time the clown you are is a combination of both previous clowns. Maybe your clowns fight for the control of your body. *Anything is possible.* Sybil can live very comfortably in this world. It can be like going to The Movies.

Chapter 9

THE CLOWNS AT THE MOVIES

Once you have met your Clown, then it is time to put this newly born clown into a new environment, some place we all can relate to, where lots of emotions are experienced and relationships occur with total strangers—The Movies, of course.

This piece can be done either as a directed piece, with very specific moves (Clowns at the Movies I), or it can be totally improvised (Clowns at the Movies II). I suggest trying both, as each format presents a different set of challenges.

THE CLOWNS AT THE MOVIES I

The Clowns at the Movies I (with music) is an exercise in hitting your mark, comic timing, following directions, improvising, and knowing how to use your environment for comedy.

Here's what you'll need.

9-1

Three chairs
Clown noses with double-stick tape
The Curtain
The Clowns at the Movies Music (Go to website: www
.findingyourfunnybone.com for a free download.)
Three Clowns

Place the three chairs in front of the curtain center stage. The
scene is a movie theater. The curtain is the entrance into the movie
theater. The chairs are the seats in the movie theater. The only re-
striction is that the chairs do not move because chairs in the cinema
are usually bolted to the floor. This can be tough to stick to. Music
starts. (See The Flip!, Clowns at the Movies, pages 147–180.)

Clown 1: Enters through the curtain, walks to one side of the row
of chairs, and goes to the middle chair. Turns and waves to
Clown 2 to enter, and then sits down and waits.

Clown 2: Enters through the curtain carrying a mimed bag of
popcorn. Sits down on an end chair next to Clown 1. Hands

Clown 1 the popcorn to hold. They know each other and relate. They share the popcorn.

Clown 3: Entrance is signaled by a shift in the music. Enters and takes his seat. Clown 3 does not know Clowns 1 and 2.

Clown 2: Gets an idea. Shows the audience that she has an idea and she is delighted to her tippy toes about it. She takes some popcorn from the bag and throws it at Clown 1's face.

Clown 1: Gets hit in the eye with the popcorn (mimed). Reacts. And then retaliates by grabbing some popcorn and throwing it in Clown 2's face.

Clown 2: Reacts and really gets back at Clown 1. She stands up, grabs a big handful of popcorn, winds up, and throws it in Clown 1's face again. Just as Clown 2 lets this big glob of popcorn fly, Clown 1 ducks, and the popcorn hits the unsuspecting Clown 3.

Clown 3: Reacts. (Anger at being disturbed. Or Joy: "Is it raining popcorn? Yummy.") Then gets up with a "Why I Ought Ta" fist or a physical reaction like "What hit me?" and "Where did it come from?"

Clowns 1 & 2: React. (Oops! We didn't do a thing, laughing at Clown 3, etc.)

Clown 3: Is about to take action, Just then, the Music signals the beginning of the film. Sits down quickly.

All: Begin to watch the movie screen.

STOP!

What movie screen? Where? Here comes the tricky part: All the clowns need to look at the same movie screen and watch the same movie at the same time. There can only be one movie screen they are watching, and all the emotional reaction to the movie needs to happen to all the clowns at the same time.

In this version, the cues to represent the movies different parts are signaled by the music.

In the totally improvised version (Clowns at the Movies II), the clowns need to be so aware of each other that they are improvising watching the same movie at the same time without the verbal or audio cue of the music or words. Whew!

The Movies emotional sequence is:

1. Funny
2. Scary
3. Horrific
4. Romantic
5. Sad
6. Exciting
7. End-of-Movie Reaction
8. Exit

So . . . The first part of the film is Funny (cartoon music [9-2]). The second part of the film is Scary. This BUILDS gradually until there is a bump/thump sound, and everyone needs to jump at the same time.

9-2

9-3

Then it goes from Scary (9-3) to Horrific to Terrifying to Blood-Curdling Horrific (9-4) until there is another bump/thump sound, and all clowns jump again together.

Then it is Romantic. Then the movie is Sad. Then it is the Chase (Exciting [9-1]).

Then the film ends. All clowns show how they felt about the movie.

Clowns 1 & 2: Exit. They can relate to 3 (for example, tweak his nose, dump popcorn on him, etc.) or not and just exit.

Clown 3: Is asleep. Remains asleep until Clowns 1 and 2 have left. Then Gets up, Reacts, and Exits.

All action must occur within the time limits of the music, using the music as cues.

9-4

The action that occurs is dependent on the relationships that occur while in the action of watching the movies and according to the emotions being watched in the movies.

Even though this version is very specific, no two Clowns at the Movies I ever turn out the same. The scenario has strict boundaries, but there is actually a lot of room for comedy creation. It develops from the relationships that are established by the clowns, the environment of the movie theater, and the emotional reactions to the movie and the other clowns watching the movies. This piece works well with both younger and older students alike.

Be sure to be aware of the environment.

A movie theater is often times filled with people. The clowns need to be aware of what happens if they jump up and stay standing, or if they go flying off their seat. Also, the floor of a movie theater is usually sticky and filled with things to deal/play with, as one of the unexpected surprises and consequences of leaving your seat.

There are many levels to doing this piece. Level 1 is to hit the mark and stay in your clown shape and character. Level 2 is to add improvisation within the boundaries of the scenario. Level 3 is to develop your clown character by focusing on the emotional reactions to the movie and to the other characters at the movies. Making a strong choice for your body shape and then experiencing your emotional reactions in a big way leads to very rich characters and events within the boundary of the scenario. Each clown part in this piece offers different challenges, and so repeating this many times and playing all the parts is great.

THE CLOWNS AT THE MOVIES II

This time the piece is totally improvised and can accommodate a large number of clowns. There is absolutely no preplanning or marks to hit. You can have a long row of chairs with enough chairs for all participating. (Or if you wish to surprise the clowns, take one or two chairs away without them knowing and watch what happens as they all try to settle in to watch the film.) Remember as a clown you are looking for a problem to solve.

This version is from Ctibor Turba. It is great because you really need to apply all your clowning skills of observation, spontaneity, strong characterization, relationship, and sequencing.

This is the scenario.

The first Clown makes an entrance. Finds his seat and waits for the movie to begin. The clown in the action of entering establishes who he is. When he sits and waits he establishes even further who his character is. He needs a moment to do this before the next clown enters.

Waiting is a glorious thing to do. You are most interesting when you are doing nothing. So many things can happen in the seemingly nonactive action of waiting. REMEMBER: NO PREPLANNING.

The next Clown makes her entrance/establishes who she is. Finds her seat and waits for the movie to begin. This clown can relate, or not, to Clown 1.

Each clown enters and establishes who she is, finds a seat, relates to the other clowns and waits for the movie to begin. When all have entered and are seated, it is time for the movie to begin. There is no audio cue. The Clowns need to be so tuned into each other and aware of what is happening, not only to them, but also around them, that they can begin watching the same movie at the same time. The challenge is to have everyone enter, relate, and begin to watch the same movie at the same time.

Psssst . . . here is a trick to help groups that are having trouble tuning into each other. It is best to be conscious of the others, but while you are developing this awareness, the following will help. It can be explained after several groups have tried to do the piece. Decide that one clown will start the different sections of the movie, and the others will take their cue from that clown's reality.

This clown must have a strong character and be aware of the environment of the movie theater and the events taking place in the movie. And it is imperative that this character develops a relationship with the other clowns. Do you know the idea that every person is walking around seeing life in his or her own life movie? Seeing reality from the perspective of his or her camera eye? Well this is truly having everyone in the same movie reality at the same time.

In addition, the duration of a joke is explored. If you play an idea too long, the movie is lost. If the idea that develops out of the relationship is too short, it has no meaning or is confusing. So, knowing the timing and being able to sense it is an important skill. This exercise is great for that.

The idea of giving and receiving can be a tricky concept to learn, not only in clowning, but also in life. What's really involved in giving and receiving is POWER.

Chapter 10

THE POWER

Who has the Power?

How do you use the Power when you have it?

How do you feel about having and using the Power?

How do you feel if you do not have the Power?

Can you let go and just go with the flow?

Is it great to just go with the flow?

Is it difficult to submit to the will of the person with the Power?

What does it feel like to Let Go?

These questions can be applied to many levels of life—personal, social, political, economic. And since the clown's job is the remind us of our humanity, the concept of Power comes into play often.

There are two games to play that explore the Power. One involves an object, the other involves a master and slave. Let's start with the object.

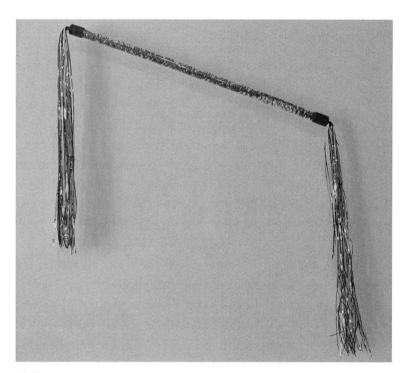

10-1

THE POWERWAND

You need the Curtain, the PowerWand (a child's baton with long flowing streamers), a two-foot-square cube, and a group of clowns. Place the PowerWand on the cube Center Stage. The Clowns all enter from behind the curtain. The Sequence is:

Clowns are afraid to come out.

They overcome their fear and enter the stage.

They see the Audience and greet the Audience.

They see each other and greet each other.

They discover the PowerWand.

They see the PowerWand.

They go to the PowerWand on the Cube.

One Clown picks up the PowerWand.

Unbeknownst to this clown and the other clowns is this Wand is a magic PowerWand. The person holding the Wand has the Power Over the other clowns. They are forced to move as the Wand Moves. Each clown whether holding the PowerWand or being manipulated by the PowerWand needs to relate to the Power, both physically and emotionally. And this relationship to the Power changes as the Clown with the PowerWand manipulates the group. So basically, the Clown with the PowerWand makes 'em dance.

This is a Discovery for everyone. How each clown reacts to Power is the challenge. Do they like the Power, hate it, try to get out of it, submit to it, revolt against it? The choices are endless.

How does the clown with the Power relate to having the Power? Is this clown a dictator, a dance choreographer, embarrassed to have the power, nonchalant, or diabolical? Does the Power Clown have the other clowns dance, and then laugh at how silly he is making the other clowns look? Or does he make them dance till they are in pain like the ballet *The Red Shoes*?

As this Clown moves the PowerWand, the rest of the Clowns are moved by the PowerWand. The Clown with the PowerWand explores moving the other clowns.

The Clowns without the PowerWand are moved, by following the movement of the PowerWand, especially the floating fringe. Eventually one or more of the Clowns without the PowerWand try to get the power.

How do the Clowns without the PowerWand Let Go? Do they let their whole bodies go under the control of the PowerWand? Do they become puppetlike? Do they only let their heads go under the PowerWand? Do they Let Go completely?

One challenge is to be moved by the PowerWand, while you are trying to overcome being moved by the PowerWand. One of the Clowns grabs or gets the PowerWand from the Clown with the PowerWand. Now this New Clown with the PowerWand explores the use of the PowerWand. Or maybe the Clown with the

PowerWand tosses it away to someone in the group or just up in the air. What happens next?

This Discovery, Exploring, Playing and Overcoming, and Letting Go continues until the PowerHorn is beeped. All Clowns freeze. Then they drop everything and exit through the curtain. The PowerWand is left behind on the cube on the stage.

This is a lot of fun. It can be frustrating and funny. The more the clowns are moved as a group by the PowerWand, the funnier it is. There is a black comedy about this exercise. It is a struggle against all odds. The stronger the clowns react to the Power of the PowerWand the more interesting the piece is.

This can be played many times with many different outcomes. It is great for character development, giving and receiving, being conscious of what everyone is doing onstage, building rhythm and dynamics, and letting go.

THE MASTER AND THE SLAVE

I first saw this exercise when the Czech clown, Polivka, used it in a workshop at the Clown Congress in Philadelphia, Pennsylvania. I was observing the workshop, and it was brilliant to watch and inspiring for me.

The elements include character variation, chromatic movements—both physically and emotionally—and going from nothing to everything in an instant. It is so symbolic of people's relationships not only to themselves, but also to each other, their governments, and any authority figure. It is Pinter, Politics, and Poetry all rolled up in one exercise.

It begins with finding the essence of two animals: gorilla and bird.

What is a gorilla? Be the essence of a gorilla—all kinds of gorillas and all the aspects of a gorilla. Be a gorilla. Show me gorillas. Take your time and explore Gorilla.

Let the group improvise gorillas for a while. Keep improvising being the essence of a gorilla even when you sense the group is ready to stop. Be patient.

It is important to push the envelope in the exploration and discovery. The most interesting work and discovery usually begin when the group has decided they have had enough and it is time to stop. This is when they lose themselves in the concept of gorilla and become the essence of the animal.

Relationships naturally develop as gorillas vie for dominance, baby gorillas play, and mother gorillas protect and nurture. Encourage using all the space just like a gorilla would inhabit the space.

Stop—Rest—Pause.

What is a bird? Be the essence of a bird—any kind of bird. Change birds and explore being all types of birds. Use the space and relate to your environment, the other birds, and anything and everything that happens.

Again, let this exploration go on for a long time. A very long time. You can make the sounds of both gorilla and the birds.

Great. Now sit down and pause.

What kinds of birds did we experience?

What kinds of gorillas did we see?

What is the essence of a bird?

What is the essence of a gorilla?

What characterizes a bird?

What characterizes a gorilla?

A gorilla is aggressive, big, fierce, family oriented, dominant, playful, and watchful.

A bird is elegant, stupid, flowing, pecking, hungry, staccato in its walking, and still.

Once you have discussed what you have seen and what are the general characteristics of these animals, then it is time to create the master and slave. The concept of chromatic expression and movement is further explored here.

10-2

You need a Master. And you need a Slave.

The Master is a bird. The Slave becomes a gorilla.

The Slave begins in Zero/Neutral position. The Bird/Master begins to move around the Slave. The Bird/Master caws (calls) out numbers from 1 to 10. Each number transforms the Slave into a Gorilla.

As the Bird/Master transforms the Slave into a Gorilla, we see the reaction to the gaining and use of power by the Bird/Master and the loss of will and power by the Slave/Gorilla.

Number 5: The Moment of No Return

When the Master/Bird reaches number 5, this is The Moment of No Return for the Slave.

The Slave in numbers 1 through 4 shows us the realization and reaction to losing control. At number 5, we need to experience what it feels like to know that you cannot do anything to stop this transformation into a Gorilla. We need to feel the utter despair, shock, submission, or defiance. And then from numbers 6 to 10, we see the Slave turn into a full-fledged Gorilla. The

10-3

Bird/Master is exploring how much fun or how much pain or discomfort she wishes to inflict on the Slave/Gorilla as he transforms.

When number 10 is hit, the Slave is now 100 percent Gorilla. Then, at a surprise moment, the Gorilla attacks the Master/Bird. The Bird needs to really be surprised and *fear for his life*. We need to feel the power and aggression of the Gorilla. The only way the Master can defend himself from the revolt of the Slave is by calling the numbers back to 1, as in 9, 8, 7, 6, 5. And with each number, the Gorilla is transforming back into a person while he is trying to attack the Bird/Master. When the Bird/Master gets to zero, the Gorilla is back to 100 percent person in Zero/Neutral position.

The two pause, rest for a brief moment, and then change places. The Bird/Master now plays the Slave/Gorilla, and the Slave/Gorilla now plays the Bird/Master. The audience watches and then discusses what they saw. Did both animals show the different steps to transforming?

For the Bird:

Did the Master use variety in the physical ways he transformed the Slave?

Did the Master use variety in his vocal commands at transforming the Slave?

Did we feel how the Master felt about having and using the power?

Was the Master benevolent or vicious or both?

For the Gorilla:

Did the Slave start in Zero/Neutral?

Did we see the chromatic steps physically in the transformation into a Gorilla?

Did we see the emotional chromatic steps in the transformation into a Gorilla?

Did we see and experience number 5, The Moment of No Return? Did we experience it in both directions?

Did the Gorilla really scare us?

Could we feel the aggression and power of the Gorilla?

Did they reverse positions well?

Did we believe one person more as Master/Bird or Slave/Gorilla?

No two people do this exercise the same. The relationship and dynamic is different every time and with every combination of people. It is a very powerful and difficult exercise to do.

It surprisingly works well with young children. They love to scare and chase each other. The dynamics of interpersonal relationships can be discussed in this safe environment of the world of animals. The Moment of No Return, number 5, is rarely done. However, the systematic transformation of the self into an animal and the relationship between animals, as well as the concept of having power over someone else and someone else having power over you, is very important for young children to see and experience whether they are going to be clowns, actors, or CEOs.

Empowerment with "in-self" or "over-self" is a vital concept, with emotions to recognize and experience in a safe environment for anyone at any age. And I'm not even touching the political, historical, cultural, and social implications of this exercise. Whew!

Clowning is deep and powerful. It requires so much multi-level thinking and multitasking. Could we just lighten up? PLEASE, someone, quick, toss me a banana peel so I can just slip on it.

Here, catch!

Chapter 11

CLOWN JUGGLING

What is the best part of juggling? Dropping the Ball.

Juggling is the only place I know where you get to blame an inanimate object for something you didn't do.

THE FIVE-MINUTE JUGGLE

Start with two mimed juggling balls, soon to be replaced with: Juggling Balls—in the soft bean-bag style

11-1

The soft bean-bag-style juggling balls come in many colors and sizes. They are excellent to learn with, because they don't roll. This saves a lot of time, body bending, and running around

CEILING

EYE

NOSE

BELLY BUTTON

11-2

picking up the balls. They are also soft, so they don't hurt when they hit you—as you try, try, try again.

To begin:

Stand in zero position.

Now point to these "body landmarks" (11-2).

Point to your belly button.

Point to your nose.

Point to your eyes.

Point to the ceiling.

These are locations on your body you will need to remember when juggling. Believe it or not, they are often forgotten.

11-3

Remember YOU ARE THE RULER, KING, QUEEN, DICTA-TOR, CEO, PRESIDENT of the ball. YOU RULE THE BALL. The ball does NOT rule you! So remember.

Let the Ball Come to You. You DO NOT GO to the Ball.

Rule 1 is to be a Ball Ruler (11-3).

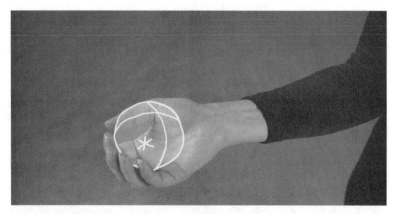

11-4

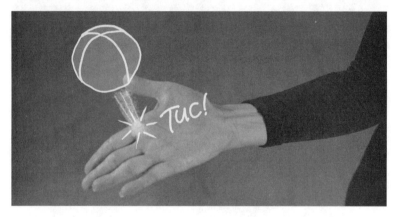

11-5

Hold the "grapefruit ball" (mimed ball) in you hand (11-4). Eyeball the grapefruit ball.

Toss it up (pancake) and watch it fly to your eye level and then watch the ball fall into your hand (grapefruit).

Keep your eye on the mimed ball. (Remember—if you don't believe it nobody else will!)

Now focus your attention on the part of your hand that connects your fingers to your palms. This is a key point in juggling. (And you don't even have an object in your hand yet!) This point where your knuckles meet your palms is the traffic cop for directing the ball. The TUC! Motion (Pancake TUC!) that occurs is actually what can give your juggling ball direction. And God knows we can all use a bit of direction sometime (11-5).

Once you have kept your eye on the mime ball and tossed the mime ball up and down a few times in both hands, it is now time to pick up a real ball—the bean bag ball. Put one ball in your hand.

Keep your elbows at your waist.

Eyeball the ball.

Now throw the ball up from your bellybutton to your eye level and let the ball drop back to you hand (which is waiting AT YOUR WAIST for the ball to return).

11-6

DO NOT RAISE YOUR HAND TO CATCH THE BALL LET THE BALL COME TO YOU. After all YOU RULE THE BALL.

Repeat this a couple of times with one hand. Good.

Now if you miss the ball and it FALLS. Thank your lucky stars, 'cause you get to pick it up and point your finger at it and scold it in a loud clown nononononono! (11-6). Then repeat the toss.

11-7

If you succeed, you get to say TAH DAH! If your ball had the nerve to escape again, then try another approach. Maybe a kiss this time will work better than a scolding? (11-7).

(Rule 2: To be a good ruler, you have to try a variety of approaches to get your point across and get the ball to do what you want it to do [11-6 and 11-7].)

Next, throw the ball from one hand through your belly button to the other hand. Keep your eyeball on the ball and catch it. Repeat throwing the ball from one hand to the next several times.

Great.

Time for the X.

THE X THROW

Take your elbows and have them kiss each other. Then cross your arms and hands fixing the point of your elbows together. This creates an X with your hands resting just at your ears, eye-

11-8

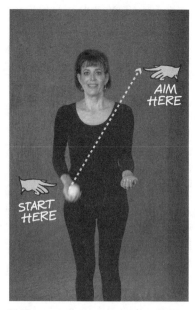

11-9

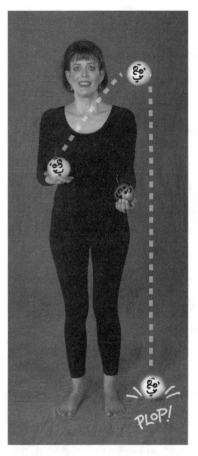

11-10   **11-11**

ball level (11-8). This is the exact route and location the ball needs to pass through on its journey to your other hand (11-9).

This is a basic throw that you will need to repeat in many variations and it is the basis for any juggling toss. Place one ball in each hand. Start with one hand (right) and toss the ball to your left ear at your eye level. Then let it fall—PLOP (11-10). Wait to hear the Plop sound before you toss the other ball (11-11). Once the ball has Plopped, then repeat the same ball toss with the other hand (left.)

Be Sure to Listen for the Plop.

Now pick up the balls and repeat this X Toss for at least ten times.

Remember to make a perfect X and take the time to listen for the Plopping balls.

THE FIRST CATCH

Have one ball in each hand. Toss the first ball to the top of the X. When that ball hits your eye level (11-12); toss the second ball to the other top of the X (11-13).

Remember to keep your hands facing up. Catch the first ball tossed. (This is a lot less complicated to do than to explain how it works.)

If you succeeded, say TAH DAH! If you got the gift of the un-expected, then take a Royal Ruler Moment with your ball and scold it, talk to it, or kiss it. Be sure to create an emotional tie and relationship with the ball.

11-12   11-13

Repeat about ten times.

Here are some types of throws you need to adjust and how.

11-14

If your balls are unevenly tossed, repeat until you can toss both balls the same height (11-14).

If your balls are flying too early and knock each other out—
Remember to pause for the Plop sound before you toss the second ball (11-15).

11-15

If you caught both balls without a hitch, you may be five-minute juggling material!

Either way it is time for some tricks.

THE MI MI MI TRICK

Place one juggling ball on the top of your head. Balance it there. Squeeze it down on your head (the balls are soft), then place your open hands together—like you are receiving a gift. Sing out Mi Mi Mi (11-16) and nod your head. Watch the juggling ball land in your open hands (11-17). If your ball goes Plop, you know what to do: Rule 2.

11-16

11-17

THE FOOT TOSS

Place one ball on the tip of your toes and curl your toes upward—like a cradle (11-18). Now, raise the knee of the leg with the ball on your foot. Kick the ball up and catch the ball with the hand on the same side of your body as the leg you kicked (11-19).

When you catch it—TAH DAH! (Otherwise: Rule 2.)

Repeat with the other foot.

For those who dare—try both feet. Good Luck!

So, you are already doing one-ball tricks, and it's only three minutes into it.

11-18   11-19

Thanks William Barrett, juggling King of Fools, for this clever approach!

Now it's time for . . . drum roll, please . . .

THE BIG-3 TOSS

Take three balls of different colors.

Place two balls in one hand and one ball in the other hand (11-20).

The hand that has two balls is where you START.

Ball 1 is located on the outside/near your fingertips.

Ball 2 is located solo in the other hand.

Ball 3 is located on the inside/near the palm of the first hand.

Are you ready?

BEGIN WITH THE HAND THAT HAS TWO BALLS. (This can be a tricky concept, thus the capital letters.)

11-20

Ball 1 is tossed to the top of the X and then Plops.

Ball 2 is tossed as soon as Ball 1 hits eye level at the top of the X.

Ball 2 sails to eye level at the top of the X and then Plops.

JUST as Ball 2 hits eye level of the X, Ball 3 takes flight heading for eye level, reaches the top of the X, and Plops.

Repeat this formation twenty times.

You are now ready to catch the balls and do a Cascade.

Please note: There are those lucky folks who will be juggling three balls in literally five minutes, and then there are those of us—*moi*—who took two years to be able to juggle three balls. Oh, I understood the concept, I could explain it, I could teach it, but my body was quite stubborn and slow in learning how to do it.

SO, if you are in the over-five-minute group—RELAX. You have only been doing it for a whopping four minutes. You have only just begun.

THE 3-BALL CASCADE

Take your starting position of two balls in one hand and one ball in the other hand.

Toss Ball 1.

Let it hit the top of the X.

Toss Ball 2 in the other hand.

Let it hit the top of the X.

Catch Ball 1.

Toss Ball 3.

Catch 2.

Catch 3.

Congratulations, you got Ball 3 out of your hand!!!

Repeat the 3-Ball Cascade as many times as you can. (See The Backflip!, Juggling, pages 180–147.)

Once would be terrific.

Twice would be amazing.

And three times is the Triple Crown (11-21).

11-21

For those of you who have not yet experienced the joy of the Triple Crown or even terrific—don't despair. You are experiencing the gift of the unexpected, which is a clown's dream. You are developing a relationship and an emotional connection to the ball or inanimate object, which can be a very useful skill—often times far more useful than actually juggling. But don't tell the five-minute jugglers that. We don't want to rain on their parade.

Speaking of rain—it's time to get out the Umbrellas!

UMBRELLA JUGGLING

Juggle umbrellas?, you say, but I haven't even juggled three balls yet! No problem. What is the best thing about juggling? Dropping the umbrella, of course!

You will need the Curtain to enter from and a small child's umbrella, preferably very colorful.

12-1

12-2

Hand each clown an umbrella.

With nose and umbrella the clowns take their body shape and clown 'tude.

When the music starts—yes, folks add music. Nothing like a tune to add zest to your clown and polish to your piece.

The clown enters through the curtain, discovers the audience, and shows the audience his new toy/trick—the Umbrella (12-2). The clown then parades around in a strong clown shape and character. When all clowns have entered and presented their exciting new game to the audience, they all stop, facing the audience, and raise their umbrellas high, and say "SEEEEE" (my umbrella/trick).

Then, Whoosh, all umbrellas to bellybuttons
Pause.

The Clowns twirl their umbrellas and say ooooo-heeee, oooooohhhhhheeee, oooooooohhhhheeee (12-3).

Stop

Count with fingers one, two, three, and shout out in your best clown voice, "One, Two, Three."

Then Toss the Umbrellas in the Air (12-4).

12-3

12-4

Try to catch it.

Miss.

STOP.

Look at the Umbrella.

Look at the Audience.

REACT.

Then go and scold your umbrella.

NONONONONO!

STOP.

Pick up the umbrella.

Look at the Audience.

Hold the Umbrella high in the air.

SEEEEEE (Audience, I have it under control).

And begin again.

Whoosh.

Twirl and OOOOHHHHHEEEE.

Stop.

One, Two, Three.

Toss the Umbrella.

Try to catch it.

Miss.

STOP.

Look at the Umbrella.

Look at the Audience.

REACT.

Idea.

Go and Kiss the Umbrella.

Stop.

Raise the Umbrella Up.

Look at the audience.

You are SUPERCLOWN! You have everything under control.
NO PROBLEM!

12-5

SEEEEE!

Whoosh.

Twirl and OOOOHHHEEEE.

Stop.

One, Two, Three.

Toss the Umbrella.

CATCH the Umbrella (or even if you miss the Umbrella)
TAH DAH!!! (12-5).

BOW.

Exit through the curtain.

Last clown closes the curtain.

Music ends.

Congratulations! You have just done your first Clown piece and even juggled to boot!

This piece holds the elements that many clown routines have. It is simple. It requires a strong clown character, shape, voice and emotions.

First you make an entrance.

Discover the audience.

Present your trick.

Build up to doing the trick

Do the trick and have a problem.

Discover the problem.

Relate to the audience how you feel about the problem.

Solve the problem (scold the umbrella).

Look at the audience.

You have it under control.

Repeat the build to the trick in a different rhythm
than the first time.

Do the trick.

Fail at the trick.

Discover the problem.

Have an emotional reaction to what is going on.

Solve the problem (kiss the umbrella).

Share with the audience that you are now in total control
because you are Superclown.

Repeat the build up for the trick in a different rhythm.

Do the trick for the Magical third time.

Succeed at the trick, or Fail magnificently.

Share your Victory/Magnificent Failure with the Audience.

Take a Bow.

Exit.

In general, this is a basic scenario for a clown routine. It is not the ONLY scenario; it is one that enables you to get the swing of how to structure something so that it leads to humor, makes people laugh, and is funny.

It gives you a road map to look at, perhaps follow, and then—lose the map and venture out onto your own highway.

The elements of comedy are there.

A strong entrance.

A strong character.

Real emotions.

A game, trick, gag, joke.

A problem to solve.

While solving the problem, you create more problems.

The Build to actually doing the trick or solving the problem.

Vary the rhythm of your problem solving.

Strong emotional reactions to the problem.

The cover-up to the audience.

The illusion that you have it under control.

The more you think you have it under control, the
    less you do.

The Victory against all odds or the Magnificent Failure.

The illogical logic to get to the Victory/Magnificent Failure.

The Victory or the Victory of the Magnificent Failure.

The Exit.

YOUR FIRST ORIGINAL CLOWN JUGGLING PIECE

Now it is your turn to create your own clown juggling piece. You can do it with a group, a trio, a duo—or solo.

Use scarves, balls, objects, hoops, umbrellas, clown noses, the audience, gibberish.

Add music just as you perform it and not before. (Cirque du Soleil tunes work great; they have lots of CDs from which to choose.)

You never have to actually juggle a thing. You just need to have a real strong emotional reaction to what is going on as you try to juggle and you will create a lovely clown piece.

Create the piece in five to ten minutes.

Watch everyone's pieces.

Did you SEE what was funny?

Can you Spot what was not?

Does your Eye know why?

Chapter 13

DEVELOP YOUR EYE

Welcome to the World of Theater. It is not a democracy. The
Director's artistic Eye rules.

Unless you are doing television, and well, that's another
story!

In the classic world of theater, the director's vision is the
one that is put on the stage.

The Director will tell you,
advise you and help you to find
your best performance. The Director is your guide—your
Seeing-Eye dog.

But there is one problem.
When you and the director
don't speak the same language.

13-1

Finding Your Funny Bone!

He speaks Dog and you speak English. He is barking at you to do something, and you haven't a clue what he wants. You try telling him in the best English words you know that you need help, and he keeps barking his help and advice. Or better yet, the director sees a bone across the stage and goes and chases it, leaving you standing there calling in your best English words, "Help, I'm over here. What do you want? I'd love to do it if I only understood what you want and need."

Unfortunately, this scenario happens more often than anyone would like.

So as a performer, you need to be able to see what the scene requires and do it. For those corporate types out there reading this, it is called ADDED VALUE. For those artistic types it is called craft, spontaneity, talent, and being gifted.

To develop this you need to develop your Eye. You need to see what works and what needs help and how to help it. So as you are watching these clowns do their juggling pieces, see if you saw a strong clown shape and what that shape was.

Did the clown use an interesting voice or sound? Was there a body movement or shape that you remember?

What made you laugh? How come it was funny? What didn't make you laugh and how did it come up short?

How could you make any moment funnier? Was there more humor in a situation? How could you add to it or subtract from it to make it the perfect mix?

Were you touched? Changed? Affected? Were you reminded of your humanity?

Remember the goal of a clown is to remind people of their humanity, to touch them with their humanity. Inevitably that is why we laugh at something and why we cry at other times. We are touched and reminded of our humanity whether it is you, personally, or we remember someone else who acted in the same manner. Clowning is no joke!

Chapter 14

PAPER MAGIC

14-1

PAPER is magic.

You can Mold, Fold, and Be Bold with it.

You use it every day in many, many ways.

It tears and cuts and covers.

It has the fiber of a tree.

You take it to lunch or read it every morning.

Imagine anything and you can transform it into it.

It rocks, rolls, and burns, baby.

In 1976 in Paris, I saw the Paper for the first time. It was Magic to me. Ctibor Turba wrote a clown show about two paper-picker clowns. They come through the audience and spot on-stage one small piece of paper. It's a mad dash down the aisle to pick up the small paper. Once on the stage, they discover a huge—and I mean, huge—roll of paper, covering the length of the stage. A battle ensues of one-upmanship as the clowns explore, transform, manipulate, and environmentalize the paper, until by the end of the show, they have created the moon and astronauts in space with just the paper and the air around them.

I was amazed, inspired, delighted, and in love with paper. Over a decade later, Ctibor Turba the Paper Clown came to America, and I had the golden opportunity to study with him. It was Magic all over. And I got to play in the paper, and I have been playing ever since.

It is time to take the plunge into Magic.

CLOWNS AND THE PAPER

In front of the curtain, before anyone enters the room, make a mound of paper. Get a roll of plain white butcher paper. Get as big a roll as you can. You'll need it. Then rip and tear huge pieces of paper and pile them as high as you can in front of the curtain. Make a Huge Pile of Paper (14-2). Then invite everyone into the room and be prepared. The urge, desire, and drive to get into the paper is irresistible.

Select a group of clowns (three to five).

Noses on.

Go behind the curtain

Honk the Horn.

The Clowns are afraid to come out.

They overcome their fear and cross the Curtain line.

14-2

They discover the audience.

Remember clowning is the In-Your-Face Art Form— so get in the audience members' faces if you like. They will like it if you do.

Then say hello to each and every clown sharing the stage with you.

Be sure to have an emotional reaction to each clown. Do you love 'em or hate 'em?

Then, either as a group, or until each clown in the group reacts, see the paper.

This is a big moment.

LOOK at it.

SEE it for the very first time.

HAVE an EMOTIONAL reaction to the Paper.

SHARE it with the audience.

Now build the suspense.

Look one way

Look the other way.

Rub your hands together and say, OOOOOHHHEEE, OOOOOHHHHHEEEE, OOOOHHHEEE.

Then, when you feel the moment is right, dive into the mountain of paper.

I stress here that, when I say *dive*, I really mean *slide*, as the floor is just that—a hard floor and not water! But either way, get stuck in and begin to play in the paper by grabbing a piece of it and tearing it, folding it, and molding it into an object. We, the audience, like to see the transformation of the paper into the object. So don't rush it, share it. Remember timing is necessary here in how long it takes you to transform the paper—enough to be interesting, not too much to be frustrating.

Use the object. Be sure to have an emotional feeling about the object. The audience will guess what the object is by how you use it. And they will guess by the details you use in manipulating it. It is a giant charade. Once the audience guesses by calling out what the object is, throw the paper away. Get another piece and make it into something else. When the Horn blows, drop everything and get out of there. Clowns caught in the cookie jar—oops! I'm outta here. All clowns race behind the curtain. The curtain closes, and the game is over.

GAMES CLOWNS PLAY IN THE PAPER

Noses on.

Get behind the Curtain.

You are afraid to come out.

Overcome your fear and cross the Curtain Line.

See the Audience (14-3).

Greet the other clowns (14-4).

See the Paper.

Build the curiosity.

Discover the paper.

Build the suspense.

Dive/Slide into the Paper.

14-3

14-4

NOW—here is the fun and tricky part. *Without* preplanning—I repeat, without preplanning—every clown in the group begins to play by making objects out of the paper (14-5).

ONLY this time, your clown observes what the other clowns are doing. AND the objects the clowns have made will turn into a game that All the clowns begin to play spontaneously (14-6). Yes, you read correctly. By watching and creating at the same time, you will spontaneously begin to play a game.

For example, one clown makes a ball out of the paper and tosses it up and down. Another clown makes a bat. The first clown sees the bat—Bat + Ball = Baseball Game.

So the clown with the ball tosses it to the clown with the Bat. The Batter clown swings, hits. and starts to run. Hopefully by this time, the other clowns in the group have made the connection and have made baseball plates, catcher mitts, fans, or the environment of the baseball game.

How your clown feels about playing or watching baseball will make a difference in how the game is played. The game is played long enough to establish a game, the characters, and the situation. But the game must not be too long to be boring or too short so that the audience wonders what happened. And hopefully, a twist is created for a strong ending.

14-5

Then, drop that game and start again with another clown's idea for a new game. Find out what that idea is by watching the other clowns create things with the paper, and then joining in on the new game.

After two to three games, the HORN honks. Quickly, the clowns hightail it out of the scene and rush behind the curtain. Curtain closes and the game is over.

This is a very good way to develop spontaneity, your eye, working together with others, and original clown material. There is no limit to the material you can develop depending on who your clowns are and how they relate and feel about each other.

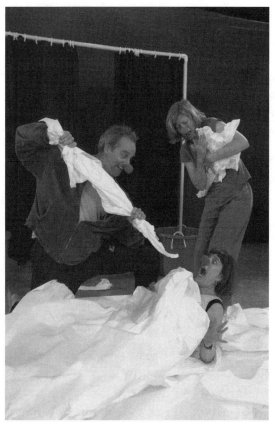

14-6

Have you ever watched children at play? They begin one game, such as ball, and within moments a cat runs by and the game of ball is dropped and the new game becomes chase the cat. They get tired of chasing the cat, and it is time to sit down and play patty cake or save the princess or attack the monsters. There is no preconceived notion of what games are going to be played or for how long. Children observe and then flow from one event to the next. Have fun with your clown creating, observing, and flowing.

Go with the Flow, Clown.

Chapter 15

THE ELEMENTS

We keep talking about feelings and emotions. But what is even more challenging than talking about feelings and emotions is showing your feelings without censoring them. This is a lifelong struggle for most people. But for the clown, he wears his heart on his sleeve. How your clown feels about something is never a mystery. It is the In-Your-Face and In-Your-Body—all-of-your-body—Art Form.

EMOTIONS

What is a feeling? Hey, let's take this question all the way by asking, What is an emotion exactly? In the words of Don Richardson, "Emotions are feelings large enough to change your life or to destroy it" (joy, happiness, fear, rage, ambition, grief). He also talked about a State of Being, which is "the feeling that results from an emotion," such as nervousness is a state of being because it can be caused by fear. When you are acting, and especially when you are clowning or creating comedy, you want to make the strongest, hottest choices so that you create the most powerful result in yourself and the audience. You want to go to the edge of the cliff and jump off into the unknown of Emotions. You want to find the emotional space "between the trapezes," as Don Richardson says. You want to find the hottest most dangerous images to play that will illicit the strongest feelings in yourself and in the audience. Yes, Yes I want to do this. I want to do this. I really want to do this but . . . but . . . but . . .

But how do you get to those feelings when you can't identify an emotion in your own body, or it is too painful or buried or hidden from you for whatever million reasons? HOW do you do it???

Try the Elements.

ELEMENTS

Elements take you to Emotions and Characters Chromatically. It's a game of percentages, for you mathematical types.

For our purposes, the first elements we will begin with are Water, Wind, Fire, and Tree. Eventually, you will discover that there are many, many more. But let's start with the basics.

To become the ESSENCE of an ELEMENT, you have to BREATH it into your body. (Get ready for an Art meets Science experience.) Just like you breath in your life, you will breath life into your characters.

To begin, find a spot on the floor and just stand there. Close your eyes. You are about to become the Essence of a Tree.

TREE

Focus on your breath. Just breathe in and out normally. Place your consciousness on your breath.

Now, you are a seed, and you are being planted in the nice, warm earth. You are being placed in a hole, and some earth is being patted over you, and you begin to burrow into the earth. As you do this, the sun above is warming you, and you begin to reach up to the warm sun.

You are sprouting roots. Tiny roots are burrowing into the earth deeper and deeper, and they are intertwining and getting thicker and bigger. As you do this, you are also pushing up through the earth to the sky. You have become a small tree. Ever reaching for the warm sun, you have branches and leaves. And you keep reaching for the sun, growing and becoming fuller and taller, and your roots are ever more entwined into the earth, getting thicker and deeper and more numerous.

Then your branches are covered in ice. Your branches are frozen, and your roots are stuck deep in the frozen earth. It is dark and cold. It is winter.

Now the sun begins to warm your frozen branches. The air is getting warmer. Little drops of melting ice fall off your branches. Your branches are freed of the ice, and they are covered in tiny buds, which are blooming into thousands of leaves. You have hundreds of more branches and thousands of more leaves. You are a huge tree now. Reaching and swaying toward the sun and the sky, while your thick roots burrow ever deeper into the earth. You are a magnificent tree.

Keep your eyes closed, and remain in your tree.

As you stand there, have someone try to knock you over, give you a gentle but firm shove on the shoulder. If you are grounded, you will not budge, no matter how hard you're pushed. If you're not grounded, you will fall over. Timber!

15-1

All you have to do to become a 100 percent solid tree is to really root. Push those roots deep into the earth. Remember, if you don't believe what you are doing, nobody will. Now open your eyes, but keep in your tree. You are 100 percent Tree.

OK, walk like a Tree.

STOP THE ACTION.

Hello!!! Trees don't walk!

You are absolutely correct. Trees don't walk, but if you try to walk as a tree—even if you don't get anywhere—amazing things begin to happen.

What do you see? Lots is going on as a 100 percent Tree tries to walk. What character do you see? What feelings and emotions are at work here? The inner struggle of trying to walk without actually taking a step creates character and emotions.

Now, you are 75 percent Tree and 25 percent Person. Yes, you could actually walk. But remember you are more Tree than Person, so you still have a lot of roots to drag around or rip out of the earth to get moving! As you move slowly along, what type of person do you see? Is it an elderly person, a proud person?

Now let's go 50-50. You can move fairly freely, but with half of you a Tree, your body is affected, and your emotional energy is different from being a 100 percent Person. Keep exploring with this percentage.

Now do 75 percent Person and 25 percent Tree. This Tree/Person can move quickly, but there is a stiffness about him, an air of snootiness or pride or fear. What else do you see in this person? Keep experimenting.

Now become 99 percent Person with just 1 percent Tree. You are almost totally a person except for that 1 percent. What does this tiny minority essence of a Tree do to this majority of a Person? Ah, there is an air of regalness, a depth in the eyes that a camera would love to pick up and does.

Now be 100 percent Person. Be yourself. Feel the difference in how you walk, breath, and relate to the world.

Take the challenge and reverse the percentages—remember what goes up in the chromatic world must come down in the same increments. What happens to these characters in the journey to return to the Forest of 100 percent trees?

Work your way back to a 100 percent Tree by reverse percentages: 99-1, 75-25, 50-50, 25-75, 1-99, to 100 percent Tree. Voilá!

What were the main emotions that the Tree carried? Pride, Fear, Determination. Did you have to dig into your emotional life and relive or rethink an event to create the memory that creates the emotion in you?

NO. No baggage. No dredging.

All you needed was just the essence of the element, experienced in doses, percentages, increments, or scales, which enabled you to create characters. These characters are not stereotypes. These characters live and breath and feel—without thinking of one feeling. All you think of and play with are the percentages of the element, in this case Tree.

Tree is the most accessible element. You do it on your feet. For the other elements, it is best to lie down. So find a spot on the floor, preferably a spot where you have lots of room to move, a spot where you do not run into other people, posts, or walls, and they don't run into you!

WATER

Lie on your back with your hands relaxed at your side, close your eyes. Focus on your breath. Just breathe in and out for a few times or quite a few minutes. This exercise takes time—lots of time—so don't rush it or feel rushed to do it. The world was not made in a day, and perhaps your Water, Wind, and Fire will take many days to develop. Just keep breathing, and you will locate their essence.

Water is a good element to experience after the rigidity of Tree. It is also an element you can relate to; after all, you need

15-2

water to live. So the odds are good that everyone has many images of water that can be immediately accessed. Begin by thinking of lots images of Water.

There are rolling waves, the ocean, the river, a pond, the drip of a faucet, the water in a glass, the rainwater, the bath water, the waterfalls—the list goes on forever. Keep Thinking and, most important, Breathing these images into your body.

This takes a great deal of concentration because you are required to let go of your Mind and let your Body take over. And we all know that the Mind does not like to Let Go of Control. But that is exactly what you must do to become the essence of the element.

Eventually—and I repeat, *eventually*—what happens is a part of your body will begin to move without you consciously telling it to move. It starts a little at first, and then more and more. Maybe your fingers flutter or your legs wave or your head bobs. Then another part joins in, and pretty soon you are moving around the floor as Water. You are rolling and floating and oozing all over. You are all kinds of Water. As you change the image of Water in your mind, the body responds by moving differently to fit the image. Before you know it, you are standing and moving across the floor as a wave or a raindrop or a tsunami. All with your eyes closed. When you stop and open your eyes, you will be surprised where you land.

You breathed yourself into the essence of Water. You became Water. You did it by letting go of all your preconceived ideas of what Water should be, and you just became the essence of Water.

What are the emotional qualities of Water—flowing, changeable, thick, fluid, drunk, carefree, relaxed, serene?

Now it is time to add the percentages. It is best to do this from a standing position. Begin with your eyes closed and breath in Water and move around the room, then open your eyes staying in Water. Just like with Tree, call out percentages, and experiment with what different percentages do to the element both physically and emotionally. Have a group watching and a group performing so you can call out the emotions and types of characters as they emerge. It is fun to see what types of characters develop when the essence of Water fills your body—and what emotions a character creates by filling him- or herself with the essence of Water.

Great.

WIND

Next is Wind. Begin in the same way as Water, lying on your back and thinking of all the images of Wind you can come up with and relate to. Concentrate on your breathing.

Don't worry about being long-winded in finding the essence of Wind. You will eventually blow into the Windy body. Let it all blow out. (Sorry, I couldn't resist.)

15-3

You will find that certain elements are easier to do for some people and harder for other people to do. I had one student who would not do Fire. She related this fear to a past life experience. So the Elements bring up your fears and phobias just like the PowerMask. You can't lie or fake it. It is a 100 percent commitment to letting go of everything but the images of the elements.

Once you are able to let go, you are letting your Body take over. The Body knows. You are then free to move. You trust that your Body knows what to do. And your Body does it very well, without your controlling every move.

What are the characteristics of Wind? What are the emotions the Wind provokes?

Wind is an element that you do not actually see. But you feel its effects. So wind can get you into feelings and emotions because you don't see it; you are acted upon by it. What kind of person is a Windy person? How do these things change when you add and subtract percentages? You will find that Wind can be delicate like a warm breeze and violent like a tornado.

FIRE

Speaking of violence, try Fire. Fire is also an element we use every day. We light a stove or a match or a candle. We need fire to keep us warm. It is beautiful to watch. It is cozy and warm. But remember what your Mother said: "Don't play with fire, or you will get burned."

Repeat the breathing on the floor with images of all kinds of Fire. Fire energy is fast and flickering. Even when it is warm, it has an urgency to it that Water does not have. Once you have found Fire in your body, with your eyes closed, lying on the floor, stand up and find it with your eyes open. Burn, baby, burn! Now experiment with the percentages. Identify the types of characters who come from the essence of Fire and the emotions that

15-4

these characters flash. Fire is definitely rage, passion, and anger. It is also cozy and warm.

Then discuss what you have seen.

There are vast arrays of characters that will breathe into your space using the elements. After you have tried Tree, Water, Wind, and Fire, it is time to bring in your own element. Observe something like a guitar string or a bouncing ball; bring it to demonstrate the element, and then become the essence of it. There are an unlimited number of "elements."

All you need to do is observe, breathe, and become the essence of the movement. You have a wealth of characters and emotional expression in your every breath.

So the Elements are similar to Masks in that they have more than one side to them. They are Tools that can be used to create a wide range of emotions and characterizations. Using percentages you have a way to create a personal measuring device, which you can use to repeat the feeling and characterization on cue. As the German soldier in the TV series *Laugh-In* would say, Verrry interesting!

You add and subtract the amount of element or animal or character mask to mix just the right blend of element to create your character.

This same idea can be applied to Character Masks and Animals. For example, explore Cat with a character mask. How a cat moves. The essence of a cat, and what emotional characteristics make up Cat. Then, begin playing the percentage game. A little math goes a long vay, ya?

There is No need to have to remember those rage-filled memories over and over again until you cure yourself of the memory and have to search for another painful experience you would prefer to forget. Or think you can't feel emotions or express them because you are blocking yourself with the baggage you carry around with you—the baggage you have a problem letting go of in time for the play or audition or reading. There are many paths into emotional expression. Rage or Anger with no holding back can be a Forest Fire. Go ahead—Think Fire, Breath Fire. Go Burn up the floor, baby. Have fun while you are doing it. Anger can be Fun!

Great, so we have a world of characters filled with emotions and degrees of emotions.

What's next? Relationships, of course.

Chapter 16

RELATIONSHIPS

How many elements does it take to create a meaningful relationship? Two at least.

What you need for a relationship is a bench, the curtain, and two to four of the elements. Put all four elements on a bench, and you have a plethora of Relationships that can occur.

For example, Water and Tree love each other unless the Tree is overwatered and the relationship gets soggy. Fire and Water don't mix. They heat each other up to extinction. Wind can be friendly with Tree, Water, and Fire, until it blows up.

The relationships are infinite, and the emotional relationships that occur remind us of our humanity. This exercise gets you into thinking and looking at the world in a new way.

Suddenly, everything has a percentage and a relationship, which occurs from how one element relates to the other and in what percentage.

If you do not have the luxury of space and time, but still need to get the idea of the elements and percentages across quickly, do the exercises standing up. Have class members concentrate on their breath—breathing in and out the element as you call out different images of the element. This will get the group going. But the purist form of lying down, which is more difficult, is the best way to get the body to lead and the mind to let go.

ELEMENTS ON THE BENCH

You will need a bench large enough for four people. Place the bench center stage in front of the curtain. Each element makes an entrance from behind the curtain. Begin with Tree.

Slowly, with dignity, Tree walks to the bench. Tree chooses a spot to sit down and with difficulty sits on the bench. (Again, the difficulty in sitting depends on the amount of Tree in the person.) Let each Element take enough time to establish who it is before the next Element enters.

Maybe the next element is Wind. Wind blows onto the stage and discovers the Tree. Tree discovers Wind. How do they relate? Does Tree like Wind? Do they flirt with one another or is Wind more like a Tornado and tries to blow Tree off the Bench? Let the two elements establish their relationship before the next element enters.

Let's add Water. Water floats in. Water washes over Tree and Wind. Water discovers Tree, or discovers Wind, or discovers both. Water then establishes a relationship with Tree and Wind. Tree and Water are good together. Water nurtures Trees. Trees grow with Water. Unless, Tree gets overwatered. Wind and Water can work together, unless Wind whips up Water to giant waves. You get the picture. The relationship changes with the Essence of the Element, just like the character choices change with the essence of the element.

16-1

16-2

Relationships

16-3

So we have three characters relating on the bench. Again, wait to add the fourth element until some relationship has been established by the three onstage.

OK, it's time to add Fire. Fire enters burning up the stage. Fire discovers Tree, or Water, or Wind, or all at once, and the sparks begin to fly. Does Fire burn up Tree, heat up a relationship with Water, which brings Water to a boil, or warm Wind to a fabulous Caribbean warm night?

The key here is to get the elements to use the entire stage and the entire bench. The more pure element your character is, the more stylized the movement and reactions will be. It's more than OK to jump on the bench, roll on the floor, drip and flop everywhere. This opens up the physicality of the character, and you discover new ways to relate. The timing also develops as each element has its own rhythm and reaction time to events. Also, you have to be conscious of what the other Elements are doing to react and continue the improvised story line.

Eventually, you will realize that anything is an Element. Everything has its Essence, which can be breathed into your Body to create a character. Bring in other elements to become the essence of. How does that element move? As you breath into its essence, what emotions begin to be displayed? How big can you create them? How small? What relationships happen in the big mode? What relationships happen in the small mode?

This game can be played over and over again. The variations are endless. The characterizations and the emotions are continually evolving. It is great to add the sounds of the elements as you do this—not words, just the sounds.

Please note: The above exercise can also be done using the character mask. Begin in the Mask on the Bench, and then take the masks off but keep the mask character. Apply how these characters would relate to each other (a Wolf sits next to a Sheep or a Bear sits next to a Fish), and add the percentages for natural to stylized acting.

THE MEETING OF THE ELEMENTS

Divide into two groups. Place one group at one corner of the room and the other group at the opposite corner. Have each person pick his or her element and degree.

The setup is two Elements passing each other on the street. When they reach the midway point, they see each other, react, pass, and continue walking to the other corner of the room.

Or, they see each other, stop, shake hands, and while they are shaking hands, they transfer their Element to the other person. So Tree/person meets Fire/person, shakes hands, and Tree/person becomes Fire/person and Fire/person becomes Tree/person. It's ggHHEEE DONG! with contact. And then they cross to the opposite corner. It's great to see the transformation of element to element, character to character, emotion to emotion.

Be sure to look each other straight in the eye and react to each other. Then shake hands and while shaking hands transfer the element to the other person. So Water crosses to Wind. Stops. Looks. Reacts. Shakes hands. Becomes Wind, and Wind becomes Water. They continue to cross to the other side in their new element. Using the same partners, repeat with a variety of elements and percentages. (Please note: Character Masks work here too.)

ELEMENT ETUDES

It is time to go beyond Sound to Words. A great way to cross the Sound Barrier is with the "neutral scenes." These are scenes written specifically to be shaped by the physical and emotional choices the actor makes to create character. Apply the Elements to these scenes, and you have some great characters. I recommend *Great Scenes for Young Actors* by Craig Slaight and Jack Sharrar. These are used at the ACT Young Conservatory in San Francisco. They work very well. They are primarily two-person scenes, but you can just add the character C or D and make them more than two-person scenes. That is the beauty of them. They are like a clown entrée in that they provide just the barest of outline and lots of room to improvise real characters in relationship.

Divide into groups of two or three. Pick the element you wish to be. Then read the scene. Seventy-five percent is nice to begin with so that the element is big and strong. You can tone it down later on for more realism as desired.

Be sure to apply the sound of the element to the words. It will shape not only how you say the words but also the rhythm in which you say them.

Once you have done a cold reading of the scene, then work the scene on the Bench.

Have the characters make entrances. Use the entire space, and don't be afraid to be big and zany. It can always be brought down to fit the camera. It is much harder to bring up to fill the Albert Hall. You'll need about ten minutes to prepare your scene.

Audience members become the directors, developing their Eyes. At the end of each scene, discuss what you saw. Have the audience feed back to the performers what they understood and felt from the scene. Did you see the Elements? Which ones made an appearance? Did they change Elements in the middle? Did the Elements relate to each other? Perhaps a suggestion of a change in percentages will make the scene more vibrant. After all, we as the audience need to feel the performance, or we want our money back. So seeing and feeling where we felt the scene and where we wanted to get up and go for popcorn is important. And even more important is discovering how to adjust the scene so that we are totally engaged at every moment.

Use the Tools we have experienced to adjust the performances. Add and subtract percentages, suggest the use of Power-Mask to show your Power, or Strings to fill your Space, or ggHHEEE DONG! to relate to the other character, or a Character Mask for added flavor.

You may need to increase your element—or reduce it and become more subtle. You may need more ggHHEEE DONG! to build the relationship. Use the Clown for more spontaneity, and let your Element get more physical, and—please—share with the audience.

Oh, my God, we are actually applying the Tools we have explored in a practical and logical manner. We are becoming independent performers.

Directing 101 eat your heart out.

CLOWN ETUDE

Set the scene on a bench. Take two clown characters. Assign each clown an entire etude to learn all the lines (such as etude 8 and etude 6) from the Etudes in *Great Scenes for Young Actors*.

Give the clowns plenty of time and several rehearsals to discover the sense in these totally unrelated scenes. How does your clown feel about what the other clown is saying? What is your clown's immediate emotional reaction? What is your clown's immediate physical reaction?

Find *physical business* to make it true and interesting. Don't get stuck in one vocal pattern or physical pattern.

Be sure to make a strong entrance and exit.

These are absurd scenes. These are larger-than-life characters whose goal is to remind the audience of their humanity.

This variation will remind you of *Waiting for Godot* by Samuel Beckett or any number of plays by Harold Pinter. It is a terrific and difficult exercise for creating real relationships, emotional reactions, strong physical characters, and, above all, physical use of the space and logical, emotional physical bits or business.

This is a great exercise for creating physical business for that commercial audition. You are given lines that appear to relate to nothing, but must be fresh, vibrant, and sell the product. Being able to add a bit of physicality to your audition may be just the ticket to landing the job. Have fun!

SCENE STUDY

Pick a scene. Please pick an age-appropriate scene. It works so much better when the performer can relate to his or her character and the action of the scene. Being excited and understanding the lines is crucial for a great scene. Passion is a great source for inspiration.

Cold read the scene. Then change parts and cold read the scene again. Then decide who does which part.

Now apply the Elements to the characters and the scene. What element is your character? Apply the Tool of Elements to the characters. Apply it in not only the physicalization but also in the emotional expression and the vocal expression. Apply the Elements Relationship issues to the characters for fun and see what happens.

Yep, it's playback and payback time. Once you add the scenes, you get to apply everything we have explored to the already written scene. See if you don't find new, creative, honest, real, vibrant ways to look at the characters and scenes.

Add the PowerMask to fill your Space.

Add ggHHEEE DONG! to create Relationship, Action, Reaction, and Energy

Add Elements for emotion, physicalization, and relationship.

Add Character Masks for physicalization and relationship.

Add Chromatic Movement and Emotional expression for dynamics and real characters.

Add the Clown for spontaneity and courage to explore all the options and levels your character is willing to go.

Oh, and don't forget to add yourself and your personal expression. You are definitely the most interesting thing onstage.

Learn the lines, work the blocking, and run the scenes. Have the Eyes in the audience feed back where they were touched and where they needed to be touched. Discuss various options for adjustments. Practice being flexible and creative. Practice exploring an idea you may not like. Practice verbalizing your ideas so that other performers can accept them or at least understand them without getting defensive or putting the other performer down. Enjoy the process, and then repeat the scene with the adjustments. Know that you can find the moment, but you will need to repeat it many times so practice keeping it fresh. Whew!

Please bring back the clowns—enough of this acting stuff.

Chapter 17

THE CLOWN ENTRÉE

The clown entrée, briefly, is a clown skit. It is a scenario that developed way back in the Middle Ages when commedia dell'arte was King. It involves stock characters, which you will still find today on television and in the movies. It has a long history, which I will not get into here. It is several books unto itself.

For our purposes, I will explain it the way Ctibor Turba explained it to me in Philadelphia at the International Clown Congress, with some additions from Billy Beck.

The clown entrée was born when the circus was mainly horse acts. When the first horse act was finished, they needed to reset the ring for the next horse act. So somebody needed to keep the audience amused—thus, send in the clowns.

There are three stock characters to the clown entrée. First is the White Face Clown. This clown is the clown who is very skilled, knows what he is doing, and does it well. Today, this could be the straightman in a comedy duo.

Next is the Ringmaster. This is the authority figure. This

character has the power, and all the other characters respect it and try to abuse it.

Finally, there is the Auguste. Just say that word. It is fun to say. It feels good in your mouth. Auguste. This is the clown who thinks he can do anything, but can't do anything, but thinks he's doing it great! This is the Jerry Lewis character to Dean Martin's straightman. This is Lucy to Ricky, Bob Hope to Bing Cosby . . . you get the picture.

There are many classic clown entrées. I had the honor of working with Billy Beck, a clown who worked in the Medrano Circus when Buster Keaton was performing. He is a living library and wealth of knowledge and stories about that time and the performances of the clown entrées of that day. We created a workshop to explore the clown entrée with a group of excellent professional variety artists in Los Angeles. Each week Billy would write out the entrées he had seen at the Medrano circus. We would collect the props for the workshop and script the scenarios. The workshop began with a warm-up, and then Billy would explain the entrée to the group. Once everyone understood the sequence of events in the scenario, we would divide into groups. Each group had the exact same scenario with the exact same props to work with. After about an hour and a half to work out the scenario, we would then perform the entrée for each other. No two scenes ever turned out the same even though we all started out with the same script, props, and explanation. That is the beauty of the entrée. There is plenty of room for improvisation and creation within the boundaries of the script.

After a while we had exhausted Billy's memory of entrées. We wanted to continue exploring. This was before there were many books available on commedia dell'arte scenarios. So what occurred? We had a need and some basic skills and of course the burning desire to create new forms from old forms. This is what Ctibor Turba always was emphasizing and what Reno Goodale actually did. Reno Goodale, an excellent comedian, clown, and writer, wrote *Gnu on Trays*, a collection of new scenarios based on the old form.

The following is taken from this collection. I have used this entrée with hundreds of performers from elementary school students to postgraduate students. No two scenes have ever been alike, and no age range has failed to find the humor in the situation.

Please apply all the Tools we have explored to your clown, and enjoy.

THE AUDITION

By Reno Goodale

The Clown and the Auguste are about to audition for the circus. They are practicing before the Ringmaster arrives. C does something. A tries to duplicate it, but fails. C asks A what he can do. A says he can juggle and proceeds to mime doing this. C is unimpressed.

> **C:** To juggle, you need to have balls.
> **A:** I have my own kind of balls.
> **C:** What kind?
> **A:** Invisi-balls.

They try other things with similar results—if C can do it, A can only manage a pitiful version. C sings, A shrieks. They decide to do their dance. The Ringmaster enters. They dance for him.

> **R:** I have just the thing for you.

A: We're in?

R: You're in, you can start today. (He leaves.)

C: We're in. He's going to get our contracts. (They dance around, proud of themselves.)

R: (R returns with two brooms.) Get to work. (He herds them off the stage.)

This is the basic entrée from Reno. I have adjusted it slightly to add a bit more detail so that it can be used as a teaching tool for certain comedy techniques.

White Clown: Enters from behind the curtain; looks directly at the audience and says in her own words, "I have to practice for my audition for the circus"—she needs to establish what the scene is about to the audience.

>   The White Clown then practices a clown trick. Let's say it's a twirl. She twirls. Stops. Talks to the audience as she does a variation of twirls: "That was too slow; I'll do it faster." Does the twirl faster. Stops and talks to the audience: "That was too fast, maybe it needs to be a classical twirl." She continues to explore different twirls, sharing with the audience the plusses and minuses of each twirl.

Auguste: Sticks his head out from behind the curtain and watches the Clown twirling. He calls out from the curtain, "What'cha doing?"

>   The Clown stops, sees the Auguste, and then a relationship needs to happen. The Clown knows that the Auguste will screw up anything he tries, and she doesn't want her audition to be messed up—so a relationship ensues with different emotional choices here.

White Clown: "I am practicing for my audition for the circus. I am doing my twirl."

Auguste: "Oh, I can do that." And the Auguste proceeds to twirl in a ridiculous manner in an attempt to copy and out do the Clown.

White Clown: Then reacts to the audience how she feels about how the Auguste twirled. "Can you do anything else?"

Auguste: "I can juggle." And proceeds to mime juggling.

White Clown: Does a double take. "To juggle, you need to have balls." And shares with the audience her emotional feelings about how inept the Auguste is.

Auguste: "I have my own kind of balls." Oblivious to the Clown's reaction.

White Clown: "What kind?"

Auguste: "Invisi-balls."

Audience: Groan.

Here the performers must stick to the script and say the joke how it was written. This develops the ability to deliver the lines written by the comedy writers and also an understanding that written comedy has been carefully honed to get the right timing for the maximum humor.

Deliver the line. That is exactly what the Auguste must do with the invisi-balls line. It needs to be delivered to the audience—like a pie being thrown into the audience's face, or a ggHHEEE DONG! to their eyes, or, as actor Ron Campbell would put it, "Feed the audience, give them the food." Whatever you want to call it, the action is the same. Tell it directly to the audience.

Now this line is only as powerful as the White Clown's reaction to it. The White Clown needs to receive this line and react emotionally to it. From that emotional reaction, the White Clown then tries a new approach—just like creating the juggling clown piece.

White Clown: "Great! I know, let's sing a song." The Clown then sings in a beautiful voice a song of her choice.

Auguste: Let's the Clown establish the song, and then joins her in a horrible, outrageous parody or camp of the White Clown's song.

White Clown: Reacts to the Auguste's singing. The Auguste illicits the audience to his side, while the White Clown illicits the audience to her side.

White Clown: Tries another approach. "OK, OK. I know . . . let's do a trick." They create a trick. Or, "Let's dance!" They create a dance.

White Clown and Auguste: Dance. Again, the White Clown does a beautiful dance of any style, and the Auguste does a ridiculous parody of the dance.

During the mayhem of the dancing, the Ringmaster enters. The Entrance of the Ringmaster is very important. This is a Power entrance. It requires—and I repeat—it *requires* the Ringmaster to Fill the Space.

Ringmaster: Enters. Walks in and claps her hands three times.

White Clown and Auguste: Stop whatever they are doing. The White Clown and the Auguste must give the Ringmaster the Power. I like to camp the *Saturday Night Live* we-are-not-worthy bit by having the White Clown and the Auguste rush over to the Ringmaster and fall to their knees bowing and crying, "We are not worthy, We are not worthy."

Ringmaster: Reacts to this adoration and then says: "Let the audition begin!"

White Clown and the Auguste: In fast-forward speed, repeat everything they have done to this point.

Ringmaster: Watches the chaos and then stops the action. "I have just the thing for you!"

Auguste: "We're in?"

Ringmaster: "You're in. You can start today."

Auguste and White Clown: Go nuts with joy. I want to see ecstasy, exuberance—utter joy.

White Clown: "We're in! She's going to get the contracts." White Clown and Auguste dance around, proud of themselves.

Ringmaster: Returns carrying two brooms. "Get to work!" (Can add menial job: clean the lion's cages, the show starts in one hour.) The Ringmaster shoves a broom into the White Clown's hands.

White Clown: REACTION.

Ringmaster: Shoves a broom into the Auguste's hands.

Auguste: REACTION.

The Auguste is delighted and begins to turn the broom into a guitar and a hundred other items.

The White Clown is horrified that she is hired as a janitor for the circus and not the star. She decides to take revenge on the Auguste for messing up her chances at stardom.

Meanwhile, the Ringmaster needs to get the show on the road.

They all form a circle and The Chase begins.

THE CHASE

There is a technique to a chase. The characters need to run in a circle and appear to be grabbing the person in front of them and escaping the person behind them while keeping the distance from the other characters the same.

So not only is making a circle a tricky business, running in a circle is a tricky business too.

The secret is watching the eyes in the back of the head of the person in front of you. If you focus on them, you will be able to keep the desired distance while you create the illusion of being chased and chasing at the same time.

So the order is:

17-1 The Chase!

White Clown: White Clown to the Auguste: "Why I Ought Ta" (à la the Three Stooges).

Auguste: Takes off running like Chaplain and the Keystone Cops.

Ringmaster: Like Stan Laurel after Oliver Hardy, goes after them all, shouting "Get to Work!"

Ringmaster, White Clown, and Auguste: Once around the ring, through the curtain, and the curtain is closed.

The entrée is Fini.

IT'S A WRAP!

Congratulations! You made it through The Tour. Great job trying and discovering all these Tools:

The Performing Space Filled with Energy
Sharing Energy
The Chromatics in Movement and Feelings
The Power of Neutral/Zero
Masks: Character and Utilitarian
The Art of Mime
The Clown
The Curtain
The Power
Clown Juggling
Your Eye
Paper
Elements
Relationships
Scenes
Entrées

THAT'S ALL FOLKS!

This is the end of our Tour. It is a guide from which to work and play. Please use what works for you and leave what does not work for you. Each performer is like a snowflake—no two are exactly the same. So different combinations of these Tools will work for different people at different times.

Please Explore, Experiment, and Enjoy.

As my mentor Claude Kipnis said to me: "Please try what I am asking you to do while you are here. When you leave, it is up to you whether you ever try it again."

My wish to all of you is simple.

I hope you have found your Stupid and you now know How to Stay in IT.

Congratulations on Finding Your Funny Bone!

And in the process you have been reminded of your humanity and others.

Ho.

"That's all Folks!"

Fini.

THE GALLERY

Ctibor Turba, Bolek Polivka, Mareike Schnitker,
Tomas Kubinek, Pierre Byland

Don Richardson

Billy Beck

Claude Kipnis

William Barrett

Reno Goodale

. . . and Mr. Whimsy

THE FLIP!

Chromatic Expression:
Laughing

Clowns at the Movies

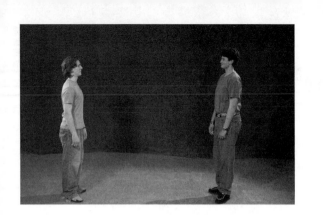

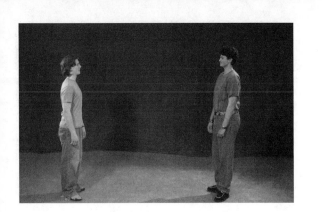

THE BACKFLIP!

gghHHEEE DONG!

Juggling

Credits

COVER

Photography: Kevin Berne, Kevin Berne Photography
(www.kevinberne.com).
Illustration: Sally Repplier Evert.
Concept: Lol Levy (www.liveartsproductions.com).
Design: Julia Gignoux.

PHOTOGRAPHY

Kevin Berne, Kevin Berne Photography: Chapter 12, 12-5. Photo
courtesy of Berkeley Repertory Theatre.

All other photos by Kevin Berne, except the following:

Nancy Gold: Chapter 15, 15-2; The Gallery, group photo.

Deborah Goodale: The Gallery, Reno Goodale.

Laura Lipper Hecht: The Gallery, Don Richardson.

JUPITERIMAGES and its licensors © 2006. All rights reserved:
Chapter 15, 15-1, 15-4.

ILLUSTRATIONS

MASKS